Ava Gardner

Ava Gardner

JOHN DANIELL

ST. MARTIN'S PRESS
NEW YORK

ISBN 0-312-06240-0

First Edition
10 9 8 7 6 5 4 3 2 1

To the memory of my Grandmother
Ellen Martha, 1893–1977.
With thanks for all those childhood
afternoon matinées.

CONTENTS

INTRODUCTION

THE DICTIONARY STATES that the word star means: 'One of the heavenly bodies, shining by their own light; a person of brilliant or attractive qualities.' The stars of the celluloid world need a little help from cinema projector lights to beam their 'brilliant or attractive qualities' larger than life on to movie screens. However, a few, a very few film personalities seem to put their lives before us on that screen so that their acting becomes an extension of themselves. One such person is Ava Gardner.

Ava's marriages, lovers, hell-raising and loneliness, her passion for parties and bullfights, plus her strangely contrasting reticence – all are echoed in the parts she plays. From *femme fatales* in the early days to the wise-cracking playgirl of *Mogambo* to the lonely, sad and drifting women of *The Snows of Kilimanjaro*, *The Sun Also Rises* and *The Barefoot Contessa*.

It has been said that Ava Gardner was the last of the screen's great love goddesses, a genus especially peculiar to

American films. At its height Hollywood had a surfeit of beautiful people. To aspire to the title of goddess, one needed exceptional looks (talent was not a prime requisite), a gift for wearing clothes dazzlingly and, above all, to exude sex appeal. Ava, with her unsurpassed beauty and earthy eroticism, caught the public's attention, held on to it and was catapulted to success.

Acknowledged as 'one of the most beautiful and exciting women of our time', Ava's beauty was never in doubt. Her acting abilities, however, were. At the outset of her career it was stated that 'she has seldom been accused of acting'. This has proved unfair, for she has emerged as an actress of skill, warmth, and – when allowed to show it – humour. She showed again and again through an intelligent approach to her roles that she was not merely a static beauty. But eventually, as time and high living began to leave their mark on those classic features, she made notoriety work for her. Ava became the woman with a past, a tired, ravaged heroine. The effect was devastating.

Perhaps, had Ava been less reluctant to make films – a task she maintained she always hated – and had the studio set-up been less geared to glamour, Ava might have become a truly great screen actress. As it is she is regarded as a great star. To have stayed the course – as she has – is in itself a worthwhile achievement.

John Daniell
August 1982

1

THE AWAITING STAR

AVA LAVINIA GARDNER, pronounced 'Ayver', was born on Christmas Eve 1922. To celebrate, two cakes were baked that day – a tradition that has followed Ava every birthday no matter where she might be. Her older sister Beatrice (Bappie) has been known to travel halfway across the world with two cakes for her sister to celebrate her birthday and Christmas.

Official handouts from the Studios during Ava's early film career always gave her birthplace as Smithfield, North Carolina. In actual fact, according to Ava, it was a place outside Smithfield called Grabtown. 'Hell, baby, I was born on a tenant farm in Grabtown. How's that grab ya?' Her parents, Jonas and Mary Elizabeth Gardner, already had five children – four girls and one boy. Jonas Gardner was a sharecropper and at the time of the great Depression lost his tenant farm. Thus life became for Jonas and Mary an endless struggle to keep their family together and poverty at bay. Ava's mother was forced to take in boarders to keep her

Ava, at three years old

family fed, clothed and with a roof over their heads. Tension between Mary and her husband developed and eventually she left him, taking Ava and her sister Myra with her. Two years later when Ava was twelve, Jonas died.

Ava was fast emerging as a strikingly beautiful adolescent, but painfully shy. Much of this shyness was caused by poverty. She was constantly embarrassed at having to wear the same sweater at school day after day. 'I only had two, the one that was on me and the other in the wash. All I wanted to do then was to die.' She proved to be a far from brilliant student and indeed showed little sign of acting ability in school plays.

After graduating from high school Ava went to a secretarial college for a year with an eye to taking up a career as a secretary. She proudly achieved a shorthand speed of 120 words per minute. With this end in mind the eighteen-year-old Ava headed for New York, and her sister Beatrice's home. Beatrice and Ava had always been close and were to become even more so when Ava became a star. Beatrice was to follow Ava around the world acting as companion, housekeeper, maid and confidante.

Beatrice at this time, however, was married to a professional photographer, Larry Tarr. He naturally took many photographs of his young and beautiful sister-in-law, some of which he displayed in his shop window. As happens in the best fiction, an errand clerk from Metro Goldwyn Mayer's New York office, Barney Duhan, saw them. He was so impressed that he told the Tarrs he was a talent scout and obtained some copies. Certain that the sultry-looking girl was just right for films he took them back to the office and then forwarded them to the studios in California. The reply was short – 'Test her'.

Soon after Ava found herself being given a screen test in New York. There was just one problem. Her accent was so strongly Southern that it was difficult for those in Metro's New York department to understand her. So the test

13

Ava, the beautiful teenager

director gave her, wisely, a test without sound. Just big close-ups of the beautiful, dreamy-looking youngster. Ava left the office ready to resume a career as a secretary. A few weeks went by before the enthusiastic studio demanded that she be shipped out to the coast. George Sidney, later to become a director, had run the test and like everyone else thought she was terrible. She did not have a clue how to act, but he was bowled over by her tremendous sex appeal. 'Tell New York to ship her out!' he exclaimed. 'She's a good piece of merchandise!'

With Beatrice along as companion Ava set off for California and Hollywood, both treating it as a 'lark' that would fold up after a few weeks. George Sidney put her through another test, virtually a repeat of the New York one, but this time with sound. It was shown to the studio head Louis B. Mayer whose verdict was, 'She can't act, she can't talk, she's terrific.' So Ava was signed to a contract. It was the usual one for a young starlet – seven years with options, fifty dollars a week to start with, raises every six months.

Ava's new home, Metro Goldwyn Mayer, loudly billed itself as THE STUDIO! In its greatest years it reigned supreme over all other studios. Metro led the field for quality, quantity, income and prestige. The roar of Leo the lion, their trademark, was heard around the world. Their films, they claimed, were the best. Certainly they were the glossiest and the starriest, and most did have elegance. Metro filmed the classics, not always successfully, but with style and élan. They also had stars: 'More stars than in heaven' went the boast. Metro's stood apart. Mystery and glamour enveloped them in a larger-than-life aura and the names on the Studio's roster were the biggest. They included Norma Shearer, Clark Gable, with whom Ava was eventually to star three times, Carole Lombard, the Barrymores, Joan Crawford and, of course, the supreme Garbo!

But when Ava joined in 1941 much of this glamour was

beginning to disappear. Many of the truly mature and stylish stars were on the way out. Garbo was soon to leave, never to return. The Second World War loomed on the American horizon, and before long such stars as Gable would be in uniform. The box-office names of the war years would tend to be mostly youthful. With a public demanding more and more entertainment the high technical standards of Metro films were virtually dying out.

Ava duly became one of the stable of pretty, young hopefuls whom nearly all the big studios kept under contract. They were useful as pin-ups and Ava did more than her share of duty, meeting visiting celebrities and mainly being decorative. She was put through a period of rigorous training, taken on the rounds of the studio and introduced to all the departments – a quick hello and then on to the next stop. Metro lavished all its highly developed expertise on fashioning a new personality out of the raw, shy girl from North Carolina. She was coached in the art of projecting the image that the studio had decided was to be the Gardner look.

Experts examined everything about her. Her figure, hair and face were scrutinised to see if she needed corrective make-up. They commented on her walk and posture, and even her teeth, deciding she should wear caps. Ava dutifully trotted them around with her but never wore them.

This whole absurd process, so memorably depicted in Judy Garland's *A Star is Born*, humiliated Ava even though she came through it all with flying colours. Her face was superb with its strongly moulded, classic bone structure – no pretty-pretty softness about it – catlike green eyes and dimpled chin. She was tall compared with many of the beauties on the studio lot, but this emphasised her good posture – and the way she moved was a delight. Her figure was sensational and they taught her how to use her sultry, natural good looks to the best effect.

There was, however, still a fly in the ointment, her voice.

16

Elocution and voice production were instigated. She worked hard at this until all traces of her Southern accent disappeared. The Gardner voice, low and husky, became as much a part of her magnetism as her other attributes, although critics were often to complain that her voice was her one imperfection, as it was with Metro's other screen goddesses, Lana Turner and Elizabeth Taylor. In no way did this prove a stumbling block in their rise to movie stardom. After all, their main requirement was to exude Metro's brand of sex appeal. Powdered, painted and dressed, Ava became the standard Metro starlet, sleek, beautiful and well-groomed, while her individual personality was firmly suppressed. The publicity department helped in this illusion: Smithfield was to be her place of birth, and the story went that she had been a model before coming to Hollywood. Ava Gardner was not her real name, they insisted, but a studio fabrication, and up to the present day it is often stated that Ava's real name is Lucy Johnson!

Metro had taught her all the tricks of the trade ready for the day she would hopefully become a star. Some achieved it overnight, but in Ava's case it was to be a very gradual process. For despite all the glamourising, Metro did not seem to recognise her star potential. She was not exactly rushed into important roles and spent a considerable time loafing around the studios, taking drama lessons, and of course posing for the inevitable pin-ups. It was rumoured that she did more than four hundred different poses in front of the stills camera in one day, all in differing costumes, mostly swim-suits that most definitely did not get wet. One fetching black lace number with bejewelled straps seems to have done service for Jean Harlow, Esther Williams, Ava and, as late as 1957, for a young lady named Marjorie-Hellen.

Ava was called on to do this 'leg art', as it was fondly called, with monotonous regularity. Turner and Taylor were never used in the same way: Lana was Metro's most glamorous female star and leg shots of her were kept to a minimum. The poses continued as late as 1955; she would often complain about this, finding it faintly disgusting, but having come this far she would put up with it, if that was the way to become a screen actress.

After a year of waiting in the wings Ava was given a bit part. She was unbilled, and it amounted to little more than being an extra. Her earliest reported appearance was in a Pete Smith comedy short, *Fancy Answers* (1941). It has been said that she also appeared in the Mickey Rooney – Judy Garland opus *Babes on Broadway* (1942) and an Our Gang comedy *Mighty Lak a Goat*. None of these roles has been substantiated and her first real screen appearance has always been given as the Norma Shearer film *We Were Dancing* (1942). Between this film and up to 1945 Ava's screen appearances were as an extra or in minor featured roles.

We Were Dancing also proved to be the end of Shearer's career at Metro. She had been Queen of the studio lot. Her appearances were events on a par with Garbo. Married to Irving Thalberg, one of Metro's top producers, she had had the pick of film roles. After his untimely death it was rumoured that Metro wished to get rid of her, but were unable to do so because she owned a vast amount of Metro stock. She proceeded, however, to sabotage her own career, by turning down first *Gone With the Wind* and then *Mrs Miniver*. *We Were Dancing* just was not good enough. After one more dire film *Her Cardboard Lover* (1942) she said goodbye to Metro, the silver screen and public life.

With stardom still elusively out of reach, Ava hit the headlines in her own way. Not as a movie queen maybe, but more as the girl who had been wooed and subsequently won by MGM's biggest box-office draw.

About this time Ava, who, rumour has it, had said on arrival in Hollywood, 'I'll marry the biggest movie star in the world,' made the acquaintance of Metro's kingpin, Mickey

Rooney. It is doubtful whether Ava realised that Rooney was the biggest star – along with Judy Garland – when she made her remark. At the time Ava appeared on the scene, the youthful Rooney and Garland were already being overworked by the studio in their tremendous successful *Andy Hardy* series.

Mickey Rooney was a great all-rounder, he was both a comic and dramatic actor, could sing, dance, beat the drums and do acrobatics, indeed anything his trade demanded. He was also rich, and a great lady-fancier. Despite being only five foot three, he seemed to have a penchant for tall girls. So naturally, when the tall, slender brunette passed by, Mickey's head swivelled in her direction and he just had to date her. Rooney was to say, 'What was there left for me at twenty? What was there left for me to do? Try marriage. That was where my drive pushed me next. My drive and the beauty of Ava Gardner.'

Mickey and Ava's first meeting on the set of *Babes on Broadway* had been bizarre to say the least. Her first sight of him was of a short man, boy really, in drag. Mickey was all dolled up as Carmen Miranda, complete with platformed shoes and hat laden with fruit. Ava, it seems, was none too impressed and at first, though flattered, refused his attentions. But Mickey was not put off, and very reluctantly Ava accepted her first date with him.

Soon they were dating frequently, being seen together at premières and on the nightclub circuit. Naturally Mickey liked to swank and show off the beauty at his side. 'There wasn't a minute when he wasn't on stage,' Ava said. To a shy girl from the South all this was new and exciting. She had been in the film city some months, but had hardly dated at all. It is not surprising then that she revelled in Mickey's attentions nor that the relationship was developing into something deeper. It was when marriage was inevitably mentioned that Ava was to experience her first taste of the gossip columns of the Hollywood press which openly stated that the girl from Smithfield was using Rooney as a stepping stone in the furtherance of her career. Of course, it was said, she could not be contemplating marriage to him for any other reason than that – and his money.

Ruth Waterbury, a columnist who was later to become a friend to Ava, said, 'There was probably a good deal of ambition mixed up in her motives. After all, for an obscure starlet to make it with the biggest star would have been a tremendous coup for her. But it would be completely wrong to say that she used Mickey.' Rooney himself said, 'Ava was rather naive and unpossessed of fierce ambition . . . We were a couple of kids, not conspirators.'

Ava, still the shy, sensitive girl, was hurt and bewildered by the cruelty of the gossip that surrounded her and she could not understand it. Her career meant nothing to her: all she wanted to do was to become Mickey's wife and settle down to a married life. Everyone seemed to oppose the match, not least Metro. When Mickey and Ava dutifully told them of their plans, the Studio held up their hands in horror. The pitfalls of their union were explained in great length. Ava was told that Mickey needed a stronger mate at his side and Louis B. Mayer himself was harsh with the trembling young girl who stood before him in his vast office. 'Once he gets into your pants,' he warned her angrily, 'he'll be tired of you and he'll chase after some other broad.'

The Studio's reaction towards Mickey was even stronger: he was their top investment, he made a lot of money for them, and also for himself. How would his fans react? They would not take too kindly to their perennially eligible batchelor being married. Would they like their idol belonging exclusively to someone else?

Ava and Mickey weathered all this by ignoring the gossip and warnings, and from this experience Ava's dislike and suspicion of newspapermen and anyone who dared intrude on her private life began. She also realised that no matter how big your name was, to the studio you were only a piece of merchandise. This embittered Ava and her attitude towards Metro, inwardly, became ambivalent.

The two were married on 10 January 1942. The wedding was kept quiet and the ceremony performed by the Reverend Glenn H. Lutz in a small white Presbyterian church in the town of Ballard. Ava wore a blue costume, her only flowers a corsage of orchids. She regretted not being able to afford a white wedding dress, and had absolutely refused to approach Mickey for it.

Their wedding night was fraught. All Ava's sexual tension would become apparent and Mickey, equally nervous despite his sexual experience, put his pyjamas on back to front, becoming entangled in them. Their nervousness finally overcome, Mickey was to find that his beautiful wife was a virgin.

The honeymoon was often a lonely one for Ava as Mickey spent much of it golfing. The biggest highlight came at the end when, after a quick promotional tour for Rooney's latest *Andy Hardy* film, the couple dined with President and Mrs Roosevelt at the White House.

Ava has said of her wedding, 'We were just a couple of kids. An MGM agent even went along with us on honeymoon and gave Mickey a dollar to buy me a soda.'

They returned to Los Angeles and set up home in a drab, unpretentious apartment on Wilshire Boulevard.

Mickey's life proved to be completely different from anything Ava had ever experienced. His family were always very close to him and, like Mickey, were all obsessed with the theatre. Mickey was mostly preoccupied by his career and his friends, all of whom originated from his batchelor days. Ava tended by nature to be possessive and disliked sharing her husband with family, friends and career. She constantly hoped he would settle down to a home life where she could be the perfect wife. But he still preferred the kind of life he had enjoyed before marriage. As the young couple began to draw apart, Mickey, thinking that his wife's stagnating career was possibly the cause of her moodiness, tried his best to promote her career at the Studio. But all she got was unbilled bit parts in pictures, with some titles that tell it all: *Joe Smith American, This Time for Keeps, Kid Glove Killer, Hitler's Madman, Sunday Punch* and *Pilot No.5* and, when on loan to Monogram Pictures, *Ghosts on the Loose.* None helped her career and most are forgotten now.

The relationship between the Rooneys was reaching an all-time low; their marriage was disintegrating rapidly. On one occasion Mickey went to a party leaving Ava to sulk alone. He returned several days later, in a drunken state, and Ava ended up throwing things at him. Again, after being left to return from a party alone, she attacked the furniture in their apartment with a knife. Ava had suffered severe stomach pains from a child and now, when they became so acute that she was rushed to hospital for an appendicitis operation, Mickey did not seem to care. Ava stated that Mickey was against their having children, but he recalled that one night she screamed at him, 'If I ever get pregnant, I'll kill you.'

Later they leased a cottage in Bel Air, thinking hopefully that a fresh locale might give their marriage a new impetus. Nothing worked however, and the smiles that had been so bright at their wedding had well and truly faded. Eventually, after a quarrel, Ava threw Rooney out of the Bel Air home, and then moved out herself. She returned to the apartment on Wilshire.

Mickey would not let her alone and plagued her constantly to take him back, trying to batter the door down when she refused. Ava became highly nervous of his demands and eventually got a girlfriend from the studio to live with her. Still Rooney persisted in his onslaught on her and they were reconciled for a few weeks, before parting permanently. The marriage had lasted a little over one year.

A divorce was granted to Ava on Friday, 21 May 1943.

The grounds were 'Grievous mental suffering and extreme mental cruelty.' Ava told the judge, 'He wanted no home life with me. He told me so many times.' There was no financial settlement and in the ensuing years Ava has never repeated anything against Mickey Rooney. She constantly gave him credit for teaching her the art of screen acting. 'Mickey showed me how to walk, how to stand, what to do with my hands, how to ignore the camera. If I ever do anything big, I'll owe it to Mickey.'

The day after her divorce, Ava received the news that her mother, after a long illness, had died of breast cancer. It was a blow that was to leave its scars. She still plodded on with her career, seductively gowned in a series of bit parts in dull and witless films, like *Reunion in France, Du Barry was a Lady, Music for Millions, Young Ideas, Lost Angel*, a minute part as a hat-check girl, and then *Swing Fever*. She resented every one of them. Finally she was given a speaking part and was pushed up the cast list to fifth place.

The film was one in a series of Dr Gillespie stories entitled *Three Men in White* (1944). Ava was used predictably, to seduce young intern, male lead Van Johnson. She gave a good account of herself in this minor role, easily outshining her fellow seductress, Marilyn Maxwell.

Men were beginning to find the Gardner allure decidedly unsettling, and some of the trade papers were enthusiastic, describing Maxwell and Gardner as 'two of the smoothest young sirens to be found', but although the trade press and public were beginning to warm to Ava, MGM did not follow it up and she was pushed down the cast list again in three dull and easily forgettable movies.

In *Maisie Goes to Reno* she played a divorcée, then in *Blonde Fever*, she was given a very small part as, naturally, a *femme fatale*.

She was then promoted up the cast list again to third in what was to be her last minor role. *She Went to the Races* (1945) was a mildly entertaining comedy about a group of

Ava, James Craig, Frances Gifford in She Went
to the Races, *1945*

professors who succeed in perfecting a foolproof system of picking horserace winners. It starred James Craig and Edmund Gwenn and was geared to the latter's quiet comedy talents. Ava as a scheming brunette had little to do. However, of the three films it was probably the best. Summing it up a critic wrote, 'They all do as well as possible under the circumstances.' Of this period Ava remarked, 'I was green as grass about everything. Half my time on the set I was trying not to cry. Because I didn't know how to do what they wanted I'd get sulky.'

Privately the ex-Mrs Rooney was prey to the wolves of Hollywood, but she managed to stave them off. Perhaps out of loneliness, and a feeling that her divorce had perhaps been a mistake, she began dating Mickey again. There was serious talk of them getting together again, but when Rooney was drafted into the armed forces she quietly asked him not to get in touch with her again. Rooney, still obsessed with Ava, joined the army frustrated and miserable.

At this time Ava was to come into the orbit of Howard Hughes, America's most elusive and eligible bachelor, and also one of the wealthiest. Hughes, like most men, was smitten by Ava's beauty and went to great lengths to meet her. When he arranged to sit next to her at a dinner party, Ava was unaware that the thin dark man she was partnering was the great Howard Hughes. In any case, she was uninterested in Hughes – or any man.

Hughes persisted, however, and ultimately they formed a relationship. Ava was showered with gifts and taken on trips in his private plane to Mexico. At first it was all very exciting and great fun for Ava, but would soon pall. To test his professed love for her she requested, a friend recalled, a tub of orange ice-cream, hard to come by at that time during the war, even in America, the land of plenty. Within two hours a limousine drew up at her door, a chauffeur rang the bell and presented Ava with her tub of orange ice-cream. It was as large as a waste-basket and Ava screamed.

Hughes, tall and painfully thin, neurotic about his health, and obsessively fearful of germs, was described by those close to him in the 1940s as a thoroughly boring man. He had no interest in world affairs or culture and his conversation centred around his business and women's breasts.

His appetite for women was healthy, and he dated many beautiful women, installing them in various apartments around Los Angeles. He shared Ava's possessiveness which provoked quarrels between them, and she soon became bored with the affair. During one argument, when Hughes' slapped her around, she knocked him cold with a copper based ashtray. Though the affair had cooled, Hughes interest in Ava continued and he set spies to report her every move. This spying continued well into the 1950s, with Ava at one point inviting the fellow into her home so that he could do his spying from the inside. Her interest in Hughes had finished, but during his lifetime he remained a great admirer and a good friend. His homes and private planes were always at Ava's disposal whenever she wanted them.

'He makes it easy for you when you want ease,' she said. 'Press a button and there's a plane ready to take you anywhere in the world; another button and there's a hotel suite waiting for you . . . He's just the ticket for a girl like me – from the Deep South and lazy.'

From the simple farm girl leading a quiet life Ava was changing into a night person. The fashionable nightclubs of Hollywood's Sunset Strip saw a lot of her in 1945, often at a party that included Lana Turner, or simply by herself. She dated frequently, and friends said that she was discovering that drink could dull the torments with which she constantly plagued herself and appease the lack of fulfilment or satisfaction she found in relationships. And it helped to ease her fears about a career for which she seemed unfit. So she drank, though she would always declare that she disliked the taste.

The nightlife accelerated and did prove providential, for she was spotted at a club by screen writer Philip Yordon. They became friends, though it would be short lived, neither having much in common. Yordon was engaged in writing *Whistle Stop* (1945) for United Artists, and considered Ava for the female lead. Metro agreed to the loan and she found herself working at United alongside George Raft, Victor McLaglen and Tom Conway. It was to be the chance Ava needed and after this film she could no longer be looked

With George Raft in Whistle Stop, *1946*

upon as a mere starlet. Ava Gardner was on the brink of becoming 'The most exciting woman of our time'.

Whistle Stop (an American train halt) featured Ava as a girl arriving back home from the big city and trailing her symbol of success, a mink coat. She takes up with a former lover, George Raft. Other shady characters are attracted to her, and Raft is almost drawn into robbery and murder. It was a well directed little melodrama, and Ava was good in it – and her effect on the male audience at the trade showing was extraordinary. The trade press were generally impressed and said: 'Miss Gardner does her best work to date as the girl who must have her man.' Ava herself had thought that she was terrible, but was secretly pleased by the response. The national critics were less kind and labelled it 'a second-rate thriller', though most agreed that Ava Gardner possessed tremendous sexual magnetism.

Just before production began on this picture someone of interest had appeared on Ava's horizon. That someone was Artie Shaw the bandleader. He had four marriages behind him, and was supposedly irresistible to the female sex. He, like other Hollywood males, was knocked out by the beautiful Ava, and lavished all his attention upon her. After a whirlwind courtship they married at Artie's Beverly Hills home on 17 October 1945. It was a quiet ceremony with a few friends and two MGM press agents as witnesses. The bride wore a simple suit, and at twenty-two became the fifth Mrs Shaw.

Though Artie was proud of his beautiful young wife and loved to show her off, he left her in no doubt as to how he felt about her mind. He even took a pile of books with him on their honeymoon for her to read, including novels by Tolstoy, Dostoevsky and Thomas Mann. Ava, who admitted to having only read one book before – *Gone with the Wind* – read them all. Her predecessor, Lana Turner, had told Shaw just what he could do with his books, but Ava always gave him credit for her literary education. She was to become a prodigious reader, and a great lover of good paintings and classical music, an image not easily compatible with that of her publicity, as an international playgirl.

During the marriage, Shaw, a self-styled intellectual, gave her a rough time, exposing her vulnerable young mind to his idea of cultural pursuits. He was constantly undermining her confidence, and berating her in front of guests for her lack of education. She tried hard to be the cultured pearl of a wife Artie wanted, but everything she did and said seemed to be wrong. Becoming nervy and irritable, she eventually sought solace on the psychiatric couch. Still feeling inferior, she took a course in economics and English literature at UCLA. She proved extremely adept at her studies and revealed that she had a high IQ. But she didn't believe the results. By this time Ava and Artie were living as husband and wife in name only. Ultimately feeling she did not belong, she left the Shaw home. Her comment was, 'He told me to leave, so I left.' They were divorced in October just one year after their marriage. To the *Los Angeles Times* Ava said: 'Artie became utterly and completely selfish in the last months of our marriage. I was barely able to hold back my tears. He disregarded my smallest wish and he persisted in humiliating me every chance he got.'

Ava's career however was beginning to forge ahead. Interest in her after *Whistle Stop* prompted Universal Pictures to approach MGM about her availability for a proposed production of Ernest Hemingway's story *The Killers*. She was offered, against competition, the starring female lead, and Metro, never loath to hire Ava out, agreed. She moved over to the Universal studios and her most important role to date.

The story concerned the arrival in a small town of two hired killers. Their orders are to kill the Swede, a small-time boxer played by Burt Lancaster in his first film role. In his room awaiting the end, he recalls the events that led him there. The film then becomes a series of flashbacks. Ava

With Burt Lancaster in The Killers, *1946*

portrayed Kitty Collins, a beautiful two-timing moll who seduces and double-crosses Lancaster. After the Swede's death she constantly lies about the facts, making it harder for an insurance investigator (Edmond O'Brien) to unravel them.

The film was directed by Robert Siodmak, a German, and as a director Ava was thrilled by him. He managed to get the most impressive characterisation she had so far delivered. Siodmark helped her to understand the motivations of her role. He used her unique sensuality to the greatest effect. She was excellent and a better actress than had been thought. Nothing now could stop her from becoming Hollywood's most exciting female.

Ava was also deeply impressed with her producer, Mark Hellinger. She told interviewer Joe Hyams: 'Mark saw me as an actress, not as a sexpot. He trusted me from the beginning, and I trusted him. I knew he was a genius. He gave me a feeling of the responsibility of being a movie star which I had never for a moment felt before.'

Collaborating on the screenplay were Hemingway himself, and the then unknown John Huston. Both were to become friends of Ava's in later years, and Hemingway was impressed with her performance. Although the film was considered a brutal, sordid affair, it was still seen as head and shoulders above other films of its type doing the rounds. There was praise from the critics who called it one of Hollywood's top-flight thrillers. *The Killers* was to become a film classic and remains to this day more satisfying than the subsequent remakes. All agreed that Siodmak had done wonders for Ava: she was becoming noticed for her acting and not just her looks. Though it would take her some time to shake off the remark that 'she has never been accused of acting'. Universal did not corroborate that remark and, pleased, sold the film and Ava as their new sex sensation.

With all the praise for her performance, Ava was the only one who did not believe she was good, and was still apt to

take any praise for her work with suspicion and a great deal of scepticism. She was convinced that she would finally come a cropper and that the movie world would discover her complete lack of talent. The inferiority complex seemed to be getting bigger. She would tell a reporter in later years: 'I have never really enjoyed making motion pictures. I'm basically a shy person. I don't mean I don't work at films, I do, I work like a legitimate ... You know, I feel I'm giving so little to the picture because I'm such a rotten actress, that I do try to be completely professional. As I'm being paid well for it, I do the job as best I can,' and again, 'I really don't think I'm good. There is something terribly, terribly lacking and when I see myself on the screen it embarrasses me.'

Metro began to realise that she possessed some potential, and wondered what to do with her. They did not seem to need a new sexy screen siren. Their films at that period were light family entertainment, and their stars were either ladylike in the Greer Garson mould, or fresh-faced juveniles like Garland, Rooney, Margaret O'Brien, June Allyson and pert little Jane Powell. If a siren should rear her head in one of their films she was usually the blonde, fluffy, teenage bobby sox type. Or Metro's number one seductress Lana Turner.

They offered Ava a role in *The Hucksters* (1947) but, typically, pushed her down the cast list to fifth place despite her co-starring status in her last two pictures. Clark Gable was the star and had at first refused it, consenting after there had been some major rewrites. His co-star was Metro's newest import from England, Deborah Kerr. It was felt by the studio that Ava might prove a perfect foil for Miss Kerr. They were right: not only did she prove perfect, she managed to steal most of her footage from her co-stars. As a young singer awaiting her big chance, Ava brought a freshness and warmth to the part and it is considered to be her most appealing role.

(From left to right) Clark Gable, Ava Gardner, Deborah Kerr, Gloria Holden, Adolphe Menjou in The Hucksters, *1947*

The film itself turned out to be a rather long-drawn-out story about commercial broadcasting and the power wielded behind the scenes by the sponsors. As Gable's ex-girlfriend, Ava was not called upon to seduce anyone, and had to lose him to the demure Deborah Kerr. Gable admired her, and she had long had a crush on him. During a difficult take Gable reassuringly told her: 'You don't see yourself as an actress and I don't see myself as an actor. That makes us even.'

Despite a career that was on the move Ava at this time seemed to be a very unhappy lady. She had scant respect for the roles being offered her, and with her second marriage over she was thoroughly depressed. She talked of quitting films and trying for a doctorate at the University of

California. She had received a B-plus in an exam for English literature, which had thrilled her far more than any thoughts of top stardom. 'What good will money and fame do me if I have no happy home? And money and fame are all that the studios and my agent, who persuade me to stay in pictures, promise me,' she told the *Los Angeles Times*.

Universal Pictures then borrowed her as a last-minute replacement for a poor melodrama they were producing called *Singapore* (1947). Ava played opposite Fred MacMurray who was mixed up with pearl smuggling and Ava, before and after the war. The part of a girl suffering from amnesia was not a particularly inspiring one for Ava. The film, made in a hurry on Universal's back lot, was a poor imitation of *Casablanca* and it flopped. Ava moved back to her home

With Fred MacMurray in Singapore, *1947*

studio and, finding nothing lined up for her, left on a promotion trip to New York for *The Killers*. There she was escorted by the new actor Howard Duff, who was contracted to Universal. Their relationship, though punctuated by fierce quarrels, lasted from 1947 until 1949. Duff described the Ava of this period as mercurial, changeable, maddening and adorable and, like many before and since, he was obsessed with her.

As the goddess, Venus, in One Touch of Venus, *1948*

Universal requested her once more for their film version of a successful Broadway musical *One Touch of Venus* (1948). At first MGM were reluctant to loan her again, but the film they had lined up for her was delayed and after Ava had begged to be allowed to do it, they agreed.

Ava had high hopes of *Venus*; especially as it was her first comedy role, and she worked hard at her part. Naturally she played Venus, and, as a statue of that goddess brought to life by store employee Robert Walker, she slipped into the role perfectly.

Many were surprised at her sense of timing and comedy talents. However, although the film was well made and enjoyably acted, and it had been a hit on the stage, it was not a hit with the movie-going public. It could have been that nearly all of its hit songs had been jettisoned so that only three remained, but it was more likely because of its low budget and the fact that in 1948 audiences liked their musicals in gaudy colour, rather than the standard black and white. Its non-acceptance caused Universal to lose interest in the girl they had billed as their new sex sensation.

But the public had not lost interest in Ava Gardner. Requests for pin-ups and information about her poured into Metro's offices. At last the studio moguls began to appreciate what the fans already knew. That here under contract was an exciting young woman – one with a seductive shape and an unusually beautiful face – and, as they became swamped with thousands of fan letters, a star!

Ava was riding high on this wave of popularity, not only with the fans but with Hollywood's most eligible bachelors, many of whom her name was soon to be linked with. Her picture appeared constantly in the press enjoying herself on the nightclub circuit. She was still seeing Howard Duff; Peter Lawford also figured amongst her dates, and of course somewhere in the background was Howard Hughes. The image of the playgirl movie star was taking shape.

2

LA CONTESSA – THE INTERNATIONAL YEARS

In 1949 METRO GOLDWYN MAYER celebrated its silver jubilee of film production. It still boasted an impressive array of talent under contract, probably the largest of any studio in Hollywood. At least eighty names could be looked upon as star players and in April the studio gathered this talent together for a celebration lunch. Ava, sitting between Clark Gable and Judy Garland, could at last count herself a Metro star. Her metamorphosis had taken all of six years.

Metro had bought the rights to a long civil war novel called *Raintree County* by Ross Lockridge. Maybe they hoped for another *Gone with the Wind*. It was planned to star Ava along with Lana Turner, Robert Walker and Van Heflin. Then it was decided that the project would be too costly to produce and it was shelved, finally re-emerging as a vehicle for Elizabeth Taylor, Eva Marie Saint and Montgomery Clift in 1957.

Instead, Ava found herself in a film called *The Bribe* (1949). She did receive star billing however, along with

Charles Laughton, Robert Taylor and Ava in The Bribe, *1949*

Robert Taylor. The film turned out to be one of MGM's poorer products despite an impressive cast that included Charles Laughton – giving one of his unique impersonations as a repulsive, cowardly character who offers Taylor a bribe – Vincent Price and John Hodiak. Ava played Hodiak's wife, a singer in a waterfront honky tonk who falls for Taylor. Hodiak is involved in smuggling, and Taylor, as an undercover agent trying to arrest him, has an extremely tough time not to implicate Ava as well. The film did not exactly make Ava a contender for any awards for acting, she seemed ill-at-ease, and most critics hardly mentioned her, though one reviewer for a British fan magazine noted: 'Ava Gardner is better for the eyesight than any national health spectacles.' All in all the entire cast was wasted and the film sank. Pandro S. Berman, the film's producer, said of it later: 'We should never have made that heap of junk. It was a lousy picture and everyone was terrible in it.' But Robert Taylor at least had liked working with Ava, and termed her: 'A good Joe, comfortable to be around.'

Ava performing a card trick for Walter Huston on the set of The Great Sinner, *1949*

Gregory Peck, Ava Gardner, Melvyn Douglas in
The Great Sinner, *1949*

Ava was to fare no better with her next three films. *The Great Sinner* (1949) boasted a highly competent cast and should have been artistically successful. The story, of a man destroyed by gambling and adopted from Dostoevsky's novel *The Gambler*, was not a very creditable translation in film terms. Ava portrayed a mysterious Russian countess who lures Gregory Peck to the gambling tables and the distinguished cast included Ethel Barrymore, Agnes Moorehead, Melvyn Douglas and Walter Huston. The critics pronounced the film a travesty of the Russian novel, and its director Robert Siodmak disclaimed responsibility for the film.

Gregory Peck revealed his admiration for Ava, saying: 'As a person she has always been a close friend, and as an actress she is my favourite leading lady.' Stories of her reluctance to exploit her star status floated around the studio lot. She would share her lunch break with the film crews rather than take it in her dressing room. On finding a group of extras staring at her in awe, she laughingly lifted the skirts of a billowing period evening dress. Under the dress she was wearing jeans. 'See, that's what the gorgeous Ava Gardner really is,' she laughed. She told a fan magazine: 'Deep down, I'm pretty superficial.' Arthur Hornblower who had given her the role in *The Hucksters* said of her years later: 'She was a beautiful, dedicated actress and never any trouble, but later on she became cynical by her lifestyle and demoralised by it and now does not see the good things she did.'

Next came *East Side, West Side* (1949), a Barbara Stanwyck and James Mason vehicle. Ava's reaction to the script was well nigh unprintable – and her use of well chosen profanity was becoming more pronounced. She had little to do except seduce Mason and, although at her most sensuous, seemed to sleepwalk through the proceedings. She hated the film and disliked even more being used simply as a well groomed, beautiful clothes horse. The glossy pro-

With James Mason in East Side, West Side, *1949*

duction was what was fondly called a woman's picture. The story of marital infidelity amongst Park Avenue society, with Ava being murdered halfway through the plot, undoubtedly belonged to Miss Stanwyck, and she gave a polished performance, ably supported by Mason. The critics, however, dismissed it. Thoroughly depressed by the parts that the studio were dishing out to her, Ava began to rail against Metro and those around her.

Again she was put on loan, this time to RKO Studios which happened to be owned by Howard Hughes. The film was *My Forbidden Past*, also known as *Carriage Entrance*. It had originally been planned for Ann Sheridan and Robert Young, and Sheridan sued Hughes for breach of contract to the tune of $350,000. Ava co-starred with Robert Mitchum and it all turned out to be a very poor imitation of *Saratoga Trunk*, a mighty hit for Ingrid Bergman and Gary Cooper. Ava was cast as Barbara Beaurevel, a New Orleans belle at the turn of the century. On losing Mitchum to another woman, she employs her disreputable cousin (Melvyn Douglas) to break up the marriage. He accidently kills the wife and Mitchum is accused, but is saved by Ava's confession. Hughes shelved it for a year while he pondered on how to promote it. It was finally released in early 1951, and sank. These films would do little for Ava's career, but miraculously would not harm it either. She was still popular with the fans and a few of the critics.

Meanwhile, Ava restlessly pursued her nightlife, never wanting to be alone. She constantly changed her address and telephone number, and was drinking quite heavily, although she was never seen to be drunk, and if filming she never missed an early call. She would tell all who would listen: 'I'm just a plain, simple girl off the farm.' But even though she stated that all she wanted was a husband and a home, it was generally felt that she was not meant to devote her life to one person. 'Maybe I should have stayed in North Carolina, married some nice simple guy, and raised a big family,' she

*Ava having fun with Robert Ryan and Joan Fontaine
during the filming of* Born To Be Bad, *1950*

said. At this time it is alleged that Ava became pregnant,
resorted to an abortion, and that she never really recovered
from the trauma it produced, and was never to have a child.
A friend suggested that if she so desired children she should
adopt. Ava wouldn't listen, and the friend put forward her
own ideas as to Ava's reasons; it would have tied her down,
and that was something Ava resented. The opinion was that
deep down Ava was rather selfish.

Thus in the early 1950s Ava Gardner stood on the very
pinnacle of top-flight stardom and international acclaim.
Most of this fame would stem from her volatile private life
more than the films she made, and soon her name would
elicit excitement around the world. The reason for all this

interest was on account of a romance and marriage that were to become sensational. A decade of headline-hitting escapades were on the skyline as was the reason for it – Frank Sinatra.

The turbulent romance and eventual marriage of Ava to Frank had begun in late 1949. Sinatra was then still married to his childhood sweetheart Nancy. They had three children, and to the fans it seemed a perfect marriage, although in fact Frank had dated a lot of girls during this union including Lana Turner – but he had always gone back to Nancy. He had bumped into Ava at various functions and apparently she had always considered him conceited and arrogant. But her hostility melted after a meeting at the stage première of *Gentlemen Prefer Blondes* in New York. This meeting in early 1950 produced an almost overwhelming attraction to each other. Their subsequent dating in New York and back in Los Angeles became the talk of Hollywood, the rest of America, and later the whole of the western world.

Frank, smitten with Ava, did not go back to Nancy this time, and in any case Nancy had had enough. As the affair became more serious, so the newspapers went wild. Being the censorious fifties, stories and brick bats were hurled at the couple, and for the first time off the screen Ava was headlined and cast in the mould of a real *femme fatale*, temptress and home-wrecker. This was not true as Ava tried to explain: 'Frank was separated from Nancy when I met him. But what's the use of explaining that over and over? No one believes me anyhow.' Unlike Ingrid Bergman, whose affair with Roberto Rossellini virtually finished her American career, and Elizabeth Taylor who frequently upset her fans, Ava came through the furore seemingly unscathed. Anyway, she did not care.

Sinatra was less lucky. Physically he was none too impressive, being skinny and emaciated looking with a preposterous kiss curl and a penchant for wearing oversized suits and bow ties. Despite this unprepossessing appearance

he was the idol of the bobby-soxers. In fact hysteria seemed to be the order of the day at most of his concerts. By 1950 much of this adulation was on the wane, and he was not in quite such good shape vocally or financially. His relationships with the press had always been fraught and, with his affair with Ava, he was to take a battering. Furthermore, his disregard and contempt for Louis B. Mayer's authority caused the film offers literally to dry up. Columbia Records failed to renew his contract, especially galling after ten years of hit records. Finally, he was dropped by CBS television.

Frank gave up a lot for Ava Gardner. He gave up a home, his children, and was to pay Nancy a large settlement for a divorce; all this from his dwindling reserves, which were rapidly depleting through his penchant for high living and equally well known generosity. As things went from bad to worse, he was to become more and more emotionally dependent on Ava. It was fortunate for them both that she had a strong mothering instinct, for although all the abuse that had been flung at them had not alienated her fans or affected her at the box office, Sinatra had become the ogre of the affair, and would need all the bolstering that Ava could muster. At this point Metro, fearful of the consequences on their investment in Ava if she continued to defy convention and openly date a married man, loaned her to an English company for a film to be shot in Spain and London. For her services MGM would have distribution rights in the United States. As for Ava, with all the turmoil over her romance with Sinatra, she welcomed the chance to get away from America for a while.

Pandora and the Flying Dutchman (1951) cost $1,250,000, a large budget for a British film. Both screenplay and direction were by Albert Lewin. From the outset, he had Ava mapped out for the female lead and had written the screenplay around her personality. She was to play the part of a nightclub singer and playgirl residing with a motley group of socialites on the coast of Spain. Engaged to a racing

At the spring Feria in Seville, Spain, in 1950

driver played by Nigel Patrick, she becomes fascinated by a yacht anchored in the harbour, and swims out to it. On board she meets the owner, James Mason, who turns out to be the legendary Flying Dutchman. Condemned to wander the seven seas for all eternity for the murder of his young wife and a blasphemous outburst against God, his only hope of salvation is in finding a woman who can love him enough to die for him, thus lifting the curse. Pandora Reynolds is that woman.

Ava reported to London where interiors were to be shot in the studios and then on to location in Spain. This was Ava's first trip outside America, and her introduction to Spain was as a guest of the Spanish nation at the famous Spring Feria at Seville. Though Spain is now well used to celebrities, Ava at that time was the first really big Hollywood star to go there. With her she brought glamour, staggering beauty and excitement, and the Spanish fell as much in love with her as she did with them. After a few days of fun at the Seville festival she set forth to join the rest of the film company on the Costa Brava.

Tossa de Mar is one of the favourite resorts on this stretch of coast for the hordes of package-tour holidaymakers that descend upon it each year. They come to sample its amusements, nightclubs, bars and luxury hotels, but when Ava arrived in 1950 Tossa was just a small, sleepy, fishing village, whose inhabitants had probably never heard of tourism, let alone Ava Gardner. Today one can still see the yellowing photographs of Ava and the film company pinned up in the little shops and bars. For here, Ava was to provide Tossa with its first touch of fame.

During its production much publicity was to surround *Pandora*, most of which was brought about by Ava's friendships, and one in particular. Playing the part of a bullfighter was real-life matador, Mario Cabre. Cabre was famous in Spain, but to the outside world he meant little until the advent of *Pandora* and Ava Gardner. Extremely

As Pandora Reynolds in Pandora and the Flying Dutchman, *1951*

attracted to the Hollywood star, he soon became a devoted admirer. Rumours began to percolate into the outside world of a supposed romance between Ava Gardner and her bullfighter. Maybe she did flirt with Cabre, but it was not serious: Sinatra was still uppermost in her mind. Then Cabre added fuel to the fire by releasing to the press some very poor poetry he had dedicated to Ava.

Naturally the newspapers went to town with this, and the ensuing worldwide publicity brought a jealous Sinatra hot-foot to Tossa. It was rumoured that he carried the gift of a magnificent diamond necklace for Ava, and something less pleasant for Cabre. Sinatra was seen as the avenging suitor, and Cabre with his verses conveniently found bullfighting engagements far from Tossa, quietly removing himself from Ava's life.

Peace reigned, and Ava and Sinatra were again alternately happy and quarrelsome. After a short stay Frank flew back to the States, and Ava renewed her companionship with Mario Cabre. Later, after the film company had returned to London, Sinatra rejoined Ava there. Indeed, he would follow her almost halfway around the world in the following years. Whilst in London however, Ava and Frank enjoyed themselves in a city they both professed to love. Frank, with the throat troubles that had plagued him in the last year now cleared up, made his concert debut at the London Palladium, and the British fans were more vociferous than ever. The couple were fêted and invited to the top society parties. At one, Sinatra was inveigled upon to sing and, enrapt at his feet, sat Princess Margaret.

Back in the States the similarities in Ava's and Sinatra's natures were creating friction between them. Both were possessive, insecure, suspicious, yet warm, honest and overly generous. Neither slept much, being night people. They liked the prize fights, Italian food and liquor. Small jealousies and arguments between them were much more frequently being played out in public. Ava candidly said:

'I'm possessive and jealous and so is Frank. He has a temper that bursts into flames, while my temper burns inside for hours.' Ava's insecurity over her relationship with Frank seemed to stem from an overwhelming fear that he might eventually go back to Nancy. Frank's arose from a career that was steadily declining, and an affair with a woman whose own career was rapidly eclipsing his. Ava tried hard to convince him that she was less interested in her own career than his. She rushed to him on many occasions, helping him out of his moods and depressions, bolstering his flagging ego and telling him that he was still the world's best singer. She did not doubt that when he hit the comeback trail he would be bigger than ever. There had been a feigned suicide attempt on Frank's part in Las Vegas, with an hysterical Ava rushing to his side. But when he fired shots from a Central Park hotel, New York, threatening to blow his brains out, Ava quietly told him to go ahead if he wanted to and left. The whole affair was to become notorious.

Mario Cabre, Ava and Nigel Patrick in Pandora and the Flying Dutchman, *1951*

When *Pandora and the Flying Dutchman* was at last premièred, Ava finally emerged at the top of the showbusiness ladder. Her performance was generally liked, and she was so much better than many people, especially the critics, had thought possible. Beauty apart, she was suitably cold, aloof and arrogant as Pandora, and had read her part intelligently. She was also photographed in colour for the first time, and the effect was absolutely ravishing. The cinematography by Jack Cardiff was very highly praised and, indeed, his dramatically sensitive colour photography did much for the film. Lionel Collier of *Picturegoer* magazine said in his review of 3 March 1951:

> The Anglo-American production set up undertook a very difficult task when it started filming 'Pandora and the flying Dutchman'. And in my opinion the makers have come out with flying colours ... Ava Gardner adds glamour to her notable performance of Pandora, a femme fatale ... A feature of the picture is the excellence of the camera work by Jack Cardiff, of 'Black Narcissus' fame. Here's another superb technicolour job to his credit. The location is a small fishing village in Spain, and the atmosphere is exceptionally well created. On the whole, a most commendable, out-of-the-rut picture.

Picturegoer also thought it a courageous idea to film the legend of the Flying Dutchman in modern dress and yet still retain all the elements of mystery. Ultimately it would depend upon filmgoers' receptiveness as to whether they found it all very moving or dismissed it as mere fantasy. Unhappily most dismissed it. Probably, being overlong, romantic and overly talkative, it was ahead of its time. It has subsequently become something of a collector's piece, and every now and then turns up at small art theatres.

   Though Ava's star was twinkling brightly, Metro Goldwyn Mayer did not seem to have a good follow-up role. Then

As Julie Laverne in Showboat, *1951*

came a stroke of luck. The studios had purchased the rights to the Oscar Hammerstein and Jerome Kern musical hit *Showboat*. It would be the third remake of this particular show, the first film version being in 1929, and then in 1936. This time it was to receive a big budget, colour, plus all the production values that went into an MGM musical. Judy Garland had been cast as the unhappy half-caste Julie Laverne, but proved to be too ill to accept. Metro in the 1950s did not have the guts to cast the coloured Lena Horne in the role. However, the film's director George Sidney had originally wanted Ava for the part, and against studio opposition and Hollywood's most powerful columnists Hedda Hopper and Louella Parsons, who begged him not to use her, he held out for her. Ava got the part of Julie.

She liked working on this film, saying, 'On this one I really tried.' She proved right for the part, and with a return to her natural Southern accent and with the Gardner sultriness she proved excellent. She was far more believable as Julie than Garland, despite her enormous talent, would have been.

Showboat contained two of the all-time great songs, the haunting 'Bill' and 'Can't help lovin' that man of mine'. These were Julie's songs, and Ava was determined to sing them herself, hoping to prove that she could hold her own against co-stars Kathryn Grayson and Howard Keel, both trained singers. This fact, and her abiding terror of microphones, made Ava's recording session a nervous ordeal. To help, the lights were turned off in the recording studio. Not being able to see the mike, Ava sang into the dark beautifully. The accent she had worked so hard to lose now became an asset in her rendering of the songs and the studio crew ended up applauding.

Ava said: 'I really thought Julie should sound a little like a negro since she's supposed to have negro blood. Those songs like "Bill" shouldn't sound like an opera.' George Sidney had been proven right in his choice, but Metro, with a lack of faith in Ava's vocal abilities, had all her numbers dubbed

With Kathryn Grayson and Arthur Freed in a scene from Showboat, *1951*

by another singer. This was another blow to her ego and she became disillusioned. Not even the fact that her voice was left on the soundtrack albums helped to soften the blow. Ironically the albums were best sellers and she still receives royalties on them to this day. But on the film's soundtrack it is Annette Warren's voice that can be heard.

The film was, of course, a big hit, though some critics did have reservations about Ava's performance. The majority talked of her in glowing terms, and it was the turning point: from then on there would be little she could do wrong. With success and international stardom assured through *Pandora* and *Showboat*, Metro renewed Ava's contract for another

62

*With Clark Gable (left) and Broderick Crawford
in* Lone Star, *1952*

seven years. Her salary rose to $50,000 a year – not a terrific amount as she was now expected to live the life of an MGM star, and that could be an expensive business. The contract was as rigid in its do's and don't's as the studio could make it. No Metro star was expected to turn down any role offered, either by Metro or when on loan to another studio. Metro made a sizeable profit out of these loans, though the star received nothing. Ava may well have wanted to turn down their next offer despite starring again with Clark Gable.

Lone Star (1952) was not a particularly good western: nobody liked the script, and it was a sad drama to give to a big star such as Gable, whose career at MGM had been faltering for some time. Gable's health was also failing and he was in the early stages of Parkinson's disease, and, though he liked Ava, seemed to resent her vibrant youthfulness. The film's plot, concerning the annexation of Texas, was an exaggeration of the truth, and the critics neither liked the film, or Ava's newspaper-woman role. A typical statement was: 'Miss Gardner ... is decorative but not much more.' *Picturegoer*'s Lionel Collier had a little more to say:

> Clark Gable in search of his youth – that's the rather fusty flavour of this time worn western. Added to which you'll have to study American history if you wish to keep a tight rein on the plot, for it's set in 1845 when the new Republic of Texas was deciding whether or not to join the United States ... Personally, I found it not only confusing, but also rather boring. What's more, I took a dim view of the sentiment expressed in the theme – it suggests that the French and British were in favour of isolation for Texas in case the United States grew too strong ... Ava Gardner makes a good spitfire.

Finally in late 1951 Ava's on-off affair with Frank Sinatra was resolved. Nancy Sinatra gave him the divorce he wanted. She retained the family home and had custody of the children. Nothing now stood in their way of marrying, nothing, that is, except their temperaments. There continued to be disagreements and the wedding itself was also off and on. During one dispute Ava tore the engagement ring from her finger and threw it at him.

The marriage finally took place on 7 November 1951 at the home of a friend in Philadelphia. Half of America's press seemed to be prowling around outside, mainly because Frank had thrown down the gauntlet and stated that this would be one wedding no pressman would cover. Their hopes of slipping away to some unknown honeymoon destination were therefore doomed. The ceremony itself was quiet with just a few friends, Sinatra's parents and Ava's sister Beatrice amongst them. Ava, wearing a Howard

The newlyweds. Ava with Frank Sinatra (Popperfoto)

Greer-designed gown of mauve hued marquisette, looked stunning and starry-eyed as she became Mrs Sinatra. Certainly there seemed to be no tell-tale signs of the virus infection and 'exhaustion' that had hospitalised her barely a month before.

The couple's efforts to outwit the press and get off on their honeymoon proved a shambles. In the rush Ava left her suitcase containing her trousseau behind. They seemed to spend most of their wedding night trying to outwit the press, and this would be the pattern in Florida and Cuba where they honeymooned. Indeed, constant flight was to be the pattern of Ava's future life. She soon fell into Frank's way of dealing with the press, a thing that had never entered her head before. She had been well trained by MGM and was a movie star, thus a public figure. She may not have welcomed all the attention, but it was part and parcel of her career. Frank changed that. You did not have to put up with the press, need not co-operate with them. You chased them away, demanded their film or even smashed their cameras. There would be excruciating headlines in the months that followed. In fact, the three tempestuous years of their marriage would seem to be a series of anything but good notices.

But for the time Ava seemed content to be plain Mrs Sinatra. There were plans to star her again with Gable. He blocked them, mainly because L.B. Mayer had been replaced by Dore Schary as studio head, and Gable was unhappy with the whole set-up. Ava took a suspension rather than play Rebecca of York in *Ivanhoe*, feeling that the role was too unimportant. Elizabeth Taylor got landed with it, though she had not wanted to play it either. *Sombrero* was also turned down by Ava. *Ivanhoe* became a hit but *Sombrero* definitely was not.

Frank got an engagement in Britain to do a show at the London Palladium, and was shocked to find that the rapport he had established on his previous visit had now gone. At the Royal Variety Show, both he and Ava were introduced to Princess Elizabeth, soon to become Queen. Ava danced with Prince Philip and discovered the Royal Family's passion for corgies. Later Sinatra would present her with one, which she promptly named 'Rags'.

Whilst in London Ava stayed mostly in the background, seemingly on orders from Frank, and gave no interviews. This was resented both by the press and by a section of the public. Ava Gardner was a big star and it looked as if she was snubbing them. But all she wanted to do was let Frank have the limelight. Sinatra seemed to want the best of both worlds: for Ava to behave like a film star when it suited him, but, when he was in the spotlight, to stay in the background. While in London Ava played Mrs Sinatra to perfection.

This then was to be the pattern at all Frank's subsequent concerts on the continent. At a great many of them the crowds had come mostly to get a glimpse of Ava Gardner. Many times the managers had gone as far as billing her alongside Sinatra. On the occasions she did not appear at the concert halls the fans did not like it and were more likely to boo Frank off the stage, which helped to cause more friction between the pair. They returned to America and tried hard for a stable marriage, but their careers kept coming between them, Frank's still declining and Ava's ascending.

20th Century Fox were about to go into production with their rendering of a short story by Ernest Hemingway called *The Snows of Kilimanjaro*. Casey Robinson, an experienced screenwriter – *Now Voyager* and *Dark Victory*, both Bette Davis vehicles, to his credit – was engaged to rework the screenplay. Robinson has said that he wrote the Cynthia character with Ava in mind: apparently to him she possessed all the right qualities for the part. At first Anne Francis, a Fox contract player, was cast, but in the pivotal scene she looked nothing like co-star Susan Hayward, so the studio were forced to re-cast. Robinson suggested Ava, and Hemingway himself asked Darryl F. Zanuck the film's producer to cast her.

Snows was to be the big love story of 1952, and Ava, who thought of it as a worthwhile venture, dearly wanted the part. But Sinatra, at a very low ebb, wanted her to accompany him to a nightclub engagement in New York. A schedule was worked out, requiring Ava's services for only ten days. Sinatra agreed and left Hollywood without her. She worked hard at the role, playing the one great love in the life of the author/hunter played by Gregory Peck. But her final scene necessitated an extra day of filming. When told of this Ava became almost hysterical, fearing Frank's reaction in New York. Of course he was furious. The loan to Fox, however, proved to be a good move. Of the three women in Peck's life, the other two being Susan Hayward

With Gregory Peck in The Snows of Kilimanjaro, *1952*

and Hildegard Knef, Ava's was the best role. She had managed to endow her Cynthia with great allure, warmth and tenderness. She gave a grand performance, easily stealing the credits from the other principals. Most of the critics were warm in their praise of her and generally agreed that she was surprisingly good. Many did have reservations as to how Hemingway had been interpreted and brought to the screen. *Picturegoer* was typical:

> Rambling and not very satisfactory adaptation of Ernest Hemingway's short story. The whole thing is told in flashbacks, which makes continuity rather jumpy. Basically, it is a melodramatic hokum, but put over with technical efficiency. Gregory Peck as the author reveals that virility one always associates with his acting. The women in the cast, Susan Hayward as the wife, Ava Gardner as Cynthia and Hildegard Knef as the countess, work hard.

Still, the film was a box office hit, taking more money on one particularly foggy Saturday night than any other film in London's West End. *The Snows of Kilimanjaro* did much for Ava's and Susan Hayward's careers as international stars.

Back at Metro it seemed as if her good reviews meant little to them, for they promptly saddled her with another poor western. Her companions in this undistinguished venture, *Ride Vaquero* (1953), were Robert Taylor, Howard Keel and Anthony Quinn. All were adrift in the movie and disliked everything about it, especially the location, a dreary town in Utah where the temperature soared to an uncomfortable 120°F. It seemed an insult to three of MGM's top stars, with Taylor decidedly out of place as a Mexican bandit, Keel seemingly lost without music, and Ava doing her best with a poor script. Only Quinn managed to make something of it all. Had her character been better delineated, Ava would have given Quinn a run for the acting honours.

A film project in which she would have co-starred with Lana Turner never materialised. Instead, Ava did a walk-on guest spot, playing herself, in MGM's stylish Fred Astaire musical *The Band Wagon* (1953). Dore Schary, the studio boss, seemed to have little regard for Ava and let it be known that he would have preferred Esther Williams in that particular cameo spot.

However, Ava's star status was consolidated by the ceremony of having her plant her feet and hands in wet cement. This immortalising practice was performed in the forecourt of Grauman's Chinese Theatre on Hollywood Boulevard on 22 May 1952. She was then rushed to Cedars of Lebanon Hospital for surgery. The nature of the illness was never revealed, but she had been ill with various ailments quite frequently in the preceding months.

Privately, things were not going smoothly with the Sinatra-Gardner partnership. Rifts in the marriage widened and the press reported the public quarrels and reconciliations. At one singing engagement, Ava took exception to Frank singing 'All of Me' to old flame Marilyn Maxwell. She left the club in a fury, returned to Hollywood and promptly posted her wedding ring back to him. They patched things up, but bad publicity followed when Frank came home and found Ava and Lana Turner together. He believed that they were talking about him and comparing his sexual prowess with that of Artie Shaw. It was even wildly rumoured that he had found the two women in bed together. Whatever it was, it was enough to send Sinatra into a rage. He ordered them out of the Palm Springs home, calling the police when the two women failed to pack quickly enough.

Frank was soon sorry about the whole incident, but was to have great difficulty in contacting Ava, for she constantly changed her address and phone number. Finally he had to resort to placing an apology in Earl Wilson's newspaper column. It had the desired effect, and he and Ava were reconciled.

Metro finally came up with a winner for Ava. She was cast in the old Jean Harlow role in a reworking of Metro's 1932 success *Red Dust*. It was given a new location, being moved from Indo-China to an African clime. The name was changed to *Mogambo* which from Metro's publicity means 'passion' in Swahili. Clark Gable again starred as he had done in *Red Dust*. This time he was a big game hunter. Also in the cast were newcomer Grace Kelly, whom MGM hoped would be a foil for Ava, and Britain's Donald Sinden. Ava and he were to regard each other warmly after Sinden had broken through her shy reserve. Ava portrayed a good-time show girl stranded at Gable's game reserve. Kelly arrives with her husband (Sinden), both women set their sights on Gable and Grace and Ava fight a no-holds-barred battle over Clark on camera, but off the set they became great pals.

Metro launched a massive operation to film it entirely on safari in Kenya and East Africa. With Frank along for the ride Ava started working in the Dark Continent. At first she quite enjoyed the locations and stood up to any hardships surprisingly well, though she would later always assert that she hated Africa. She also refused to accompany Gable on his expeditions to kill wild game. Grace Kelly was less squeamish and often went along, and a romance developed between her and Gable. Meanwhile Ava was not getting along with her director, John Ford. She was upset by his apparent contempt for her as a person and a star. One day he called her aside and told her: 'You're damned good. Just take it easy.' After that they got along famously. Ford said later of her: 'She was a real trouper. She was unhappy over Sinatra, but she worked . . . I loved her.' At one point during the location, some officials complained that she was showing herself naked in her canvas bathtub in front of the natives. Ava's laughing reaction was to run naked through the camp in front of everyone.

Ava and Frank celebrated their first wedding anniversary on safari. 'It was quite an occasion for me, I had been married twice before but never for a whole year,' Ava mused. Actually, it was not a happy time for either of them: Frank was bored and they quarrelled constantly.

Sinatra had heard that Columbia Pictures were turning the sensational war novel *From Here to Eternity* into a screenplay, and decided that the role of Maggio, an Italian, would suit him perfectly. Ava agreed wholeheartedly and Frank set about publicising his determination to play the part. He also advertised that he was willing to accept any salary offered, or even none at all. His proposals were not taken very seriously, especially the bit about playing the role for no salary. Eventually, before leaving for Africa, Ava had to put in her own plea to the head of Columbia Productions, Harry Cohn, literally begging him to test Frank. Cohn somewhat reluctantly agreed. Frank heard of their decision to give him

Mogambo, *1953*

a test while keeping Ava company in Africa. She bought his ticket back to the States, he left, and she continued working away in darkest Africa.

The test was made, and all at Columbia were surprised as the singer's unsuspected acting abilities were revealed. The part was his and Frank promptly signed with Columbia who shrewdly squeezed every ounce of publicity from the then unusual casting, and at the low price of $8,000. Then another great piece of publicity accrued to their picture with the signing of the ladylike Deborah Kerr for the part of the adulterous wife. A happy Sinatra rejoined an unhappy Ava back in Africa. During his absence she had been rushed to London where she suffered a miscarriage, a fact that the studio hushed up. Some said she had gone to London for an abortion. Ava had returned to the film unit utterly depressed and with feelings of guilt. She told Joe Hyams later: 'All of my life I had wanted a baby and the news that I lost him (I'm sure it was a boy) was the cruellest blow I had ever received. Even though my marriage to Frank was getting shakier every day, I didn't care. I wanted a baby by him.'

They celebrated her birthday and Christmas in Africa with a degree of peace. Sinatra then returned to California to start work on *Eternity*. Ava left for London to do interior work on *Mogambo*, and then to start work on her next assignment *Knights of the Round Table*.

From Here to Eternity proved the turning point in Sinatra's career. The interest in his casting created a demand for Sinatra concerts and records, and Frank Sinatra took them on, he was on the way up again. When Ava returned from Africa and Europe he was not around, he was on tour, and it was from this time that the real break-up of their marriage began. Maybe the child she had lost might have held them together.

Mogambo was released and was another massive box-office winner. Ava was splendid, and the role of the wise-cracking show girl provided her with one of the best

74

performances of her career up to then. Many have said that this role was the nearest thing to Ava's real personality, character and humour. For this performance she was nominated an Academy Award as best actress of the year. Unfortunately she lost to newcomer Audrey Hepburn for her part in *Roman Holiday*. Other unsuccessful actresses that year were Deborah Kerr, Leslie Caron and Maggie McNamara. Ava, true to character, was pleased to be nominated, but more than a little surprised. Ironically Frank Sinatra walked off with the best supporting award for his Maggio in *Eternity*, which was also voted best picture. The film and his subsequent award re-established him as a hot property. *Mogambo* also revived Clark Gable's flagging career, and also set Grace Kelly on the road to becoming Hollywood's biggest attraction. MGM were repaid handsomely, for the film made their investment back tenfold, accruing more than $5,000,000 in the States alone.

There would be little reaction to Ava's role as Guinevere in Metro's large-scale production of *The Knights of the Round Table* (1954). This production co-starred her again with Robert Taylor as Lancelot and Mel Ferrer as King Arthur. The film utilised the massive castle set built for Metro's previous big hit *Ivanhoe* at their Boreham Wood studios in England. They shot it in colour and – for the first time for Metro – the then revolutionary Cinemascope process. If not as good as *Ivanhoe*, it was at least rousing, swashbuckling kids' stuff, and on that light level was good family entertainment. It was of course a financial success.

Picturegoer said: 'It's certainly some spectacle – it uses the wide screen superbly ... What a pity the highlights of the story have been sadly neglected ... the legend would have been much better if it had not been tampered with. The women are in the best Hollywood tradition: well groomed, well dressed and coiffured.' Other critics had little to say about Ava, though some laughed at the unlikely sight of Gardner as a nun at the film's close.

Above: Guinevere (Ava) arrives at Camelot Castle to wed King Arthur. Knights of the Round Table, *1954*
Opposite page: With Robert Taylor in Knights of the Round Table, *1954*

Seeing this film years later on television one seems to detect a sadness about Ava's performance, especially in her eyes. True she is serene and regal, and, with the way only she could move on screen, every inch a Queen. But her heart isn't in it and it shows. Maybe it was due to the way her personal life was going at the time, and to the fact that she did not believe in the role and was not that interested. Producer Pandro S. Berman explained: 'We were trying for a down-to-earth mass entertainment picture. It seemed more appropriate to use a beautiful woman than use someone who was a better actress but mightn't have the mass sex appeal Ava had by that time. And she didn't have such a huge part that it would have been beyond her.'

Back in America Frank and Ava were to see less of each other; he was more and more on the road, singing to capacity audiences all over the States. Las Vegas and New York were now his headquarters, rather than Los Angeles. Frank sang in the swanky nightclubs and played up to the girls while Ava sat and fumed, or just got up and walked out. Frank's parents, liking Ava, and she them, tried to affect a reconciliation. It worked for a while, then the petty jealousies and rows flared up again. The marriage was well and truly on the rocks. Ava and Frank seemed doomed, they hated and resented the hours away from each other and yet could not really live together. They would continue to carry a torch for one another for quite a few years; Frank would be the first person Ava would turn to for advice or comfort, and his homes were always available to her after the bitterness of their break-up had faded. They finally parted and Metro issued a statement that Ava Gardner would seek a divorce. Ava's comment was: 'Things were great when he was on the skids, but then with success he became his old arrogant self again.' Frank took the break-up the hardest. Friends said, 'Frank wasn't just in love with her, he was obsessed by her.' With both their careers in top flight, they no longer needed one another. Certainly Sinatra did not

need Ava's mothering any more, but still obsessed he was. Friends of this period recalled: 'There was Frank drinking a toast to a picture of Ava with tears running down his face, suddenly there was a crash. Sinatra had thrown the picture to the floor, he then ripped the picture into shreds. Minutes later he was on his hands and knees looking for the pieces, becoming frantic until all were found.'

Professionally Ava's popularity was at its height. Box-office magazine polls listed her as the third favourite star. She was cited as the world's most exciting woman, and voted, absurdly, as the one girl with whom American lift operators would most like to be stuck at the top of the Empire State Building.

With all this popularity Ava began feuding with Metro over terms and the parts she was allotted. The studio had planned to star her in another poor film *Green Fire* set in the jungles of South America. Luckily for Ava that part went to friend and new star Grace Kelly. This left Ava free to take on the role that would become synonymous with her. *The Barefoot Contessa* (1954) became an image the public would most associate with her, along with the tag of 'the world's most beautiful animal'.

Joseph L. Mankiewicz had written the character of Maria Vargas, a Spanish dancer who rises from poverty to fame, fortune and ultimate tragedy, with Ava in mind. To Ava, the part seemed made for her and was the one role she wanted. But so did most of the other actresses in Hollywood. Mainly because Mankiewicz had written the screenplay and was directing it – and who could forget his classic hit *All About Eve* which had made his reputation as a director. Jennifer Jones harassed him constantly for the part, and Elizabeth Taylor begged Metro to get it for her. Mankiewicz, however, only saw Gardner in the role and stuck out for her. He requested her loan from MGM, and they were at first reluctant to let her go.

She herself had raised hell with the studio, demanding to

be allowed to accept the role, pointing out that she had been the good girl of the company, doing every lousy part in every lousy picture Metro ever made. She also felt that she was regarded as a second-best contract player and now, with the announcement of her separation from Sinatra, she just wanted to get out of Hollywood. They finally agreed, but their terms were excessive – $200,000 plus ten per cent of the gross after the first million. Ava was to get $60,000 from the deal. When told of their terms she remarked: 'That's Metro, they'll louse you every time.' Of the part she told Mankiewicz: 'Hell, Joe, I'm not an actress, but I think I understand this girl. She's a lot like me.' Ava had not read the script she admitted, just the outline. 'Anyhow, I just had to play it. You know I've got pretty feet.'

From the moment it was announced that Ava Gardner had the Contessa role the interest in her was colossal. United Artists Rome press office were quite unprepared, as they were swamped with appeals for stories, interviews and

Ava faces press photographers in a scene from The Barefoot Contessa, *1954*

pictures of her. It was here in Rome that Ava began to become more and more Europeanised, throwing herself into the international scene. Thus her playgirl image was fostered, and celluloid and real life were merging in the public's mind.

The world's press could not get enough columns on Ava Gardner. They devoured stories of some new romance; rumours of dissent with her co-star Humphrey Bogart and a supposed feud with his wife Lauren Bacall were rife. Most were nonsense, but of course presented as fact, and believed by many. Actually Ava and Bogie were not great friends on or off the set, mainly because she kept herself to herself. Bogart did make remarks about her abilities as an actress, claiming that she gave him nothing in their scenes together. He also made derogatory remarks about her private life in her presence. Ava, surprisingly, bore his needling with a quiet patience. Rumours of temperament, accepted as fact by the film crew, were refuted by her complete professionalism. She was always on time and polite to everyone, and worked hard at her part despite some difficult locations in Rome and on the French Riviera. But all the same, no one ever lost their awe of her.

It was for *Contessa* that the publicity boys dreamed up the tag of 'the world's most beautiful animal'. The title stuck, though Ava herself did not much care for it, and increasingly to an adoring public she became the fictional heroine she was portraying. For the next decade Ava Gardner would be thought of as a 'Barefoot Contessa', international playgirl and beauty. She had by this time become the toast of Rome, and she began to talk seriously of quitting America and settling in Europe, probably Madrid, a city she liked. She told a reporter that she preferred all things Spanish to American. Also she was seeing a lot of Luis Miguel Dominguin, a millionaire bullfighter.

Whilst filming, Sinatra made a visit to Rome. The press were on the alert, hoping to catch them together. They were

The barefoot contessa dances in the gypsy camp

disappointed, for though Ava and Sinatra were together, they had to stay incarcerated in Ava's hotel suite; she had contracted German measles.

After *Contessa* was completed, Ava shot off to Madrid. She was then in a dispute with MGM. It was stated that the studio had ordered her back to the States and that she had refused to go. In Madrid she was hospitalised with a severe attack of gallstones. To cheer her up, Dominguin brought her a visitor who was a great fan, and would become a great friend. The visitor was Ernest Hemingway. Ava was delighted and reported as saying: 'I love this damn hospital so much I almost don't want to pass this goddamn stone. Sit here on the bed, Papa, and talk to me. I'm absolutely floored you could come.'

83

At times she was in such severe pain that doctors had to keep her sedated, other times she could be found shouting expletives down the phone to some studio official in California. She absolutely refused to do *Love Me or Leave Me* (1955), the biography of the twenties singer Ruth Etting. Probably, remembering *Showboat*, she resented having her voice dubbed again. 'What in Christ are you trying to do to me? ... I stand there mouthing words like a great goldfish while you're piping in some goddamn dubbed voice,' she yelled down the phone. Consequently the film was made with Doris Day in the starring role, providing Miss Day with one of her best movies and performances, and establishing her as an actress of dramatic ability. It proved to be one film Ava should not have turned down

Later she returned to America, and at the airport she was asked to pose for the television cameras. Someone told her that Metro had set it up. Ava exploded, 'Metro! Well I don't do TV, especially Metro TV!' She let it be known that after sorting things out in Los Angeles, she was going to live in Europe, permanently.

Shortly after her arrival in Hollywood, MGM issued a statement that Miss Ava Gardner was on suspension, whereupon Ava headed for Lake Tahoe, Nevada, and became a resident. Presumably to be eligible for a divorce from Frank Sinatra. Reports from Tahoe stated that both Luis Dominguin and Howard Hughes had been visitors to her. But Ava in true Garbo style kept everyone, especially her studio, in the dark as to where or what she was doing. She really had gone to ground in Tahoe.

Ava later revealed to David Hanna that Hughes had arrived in Tahoe with a shoe box containing $250,000. He wanted her to make a picture for him, and the money was a bonus. Ava rejected the idea stating: 'If he wanted to make a deal with me he'd have to talk to my agent like everybody else. That I wasn't touching that kind of money – not now – not ever. Not if I starve.'

On the day she was to appear in court to testify in her divorce proceedings, the place literally crawled with newsmen and sightseers. But Ava did not show up, instead she left Lake Tahoe. Although having completed her residency she could return to Nevada at a later date and pick up her divorce papers, she never did.

Ava then left on a strenuous tour for United Artists in connection with 'the Barefoot Contessa' of South America. This was actually a promotional tour. It started in Lima, where she was mobbed by thousands of deliriously excited Latin Americans, which was to be the pattern all through the tour. Everywhere she went she was mobbed and the newsmen and executives of United Artists found her in the very best of spirits. David Hanna from United accompanied her, and later was to take on the job of her publicist, and to write a charming book on his experiences working for Ava.

Only one incident marred the tour and that happened in Brazil. Headlines screamed around the world, 'Ava Gardner drunk on arrival at hotel', 'Gardner smashes furniture', 'Ava hurls champagne glass at hotel manager', and 'Ava Gardner ejected from her hotel'.

The truth was very different. The plane had arrived at Brazil airport, and again thousands had turned up to meet her. They turned into an unruly mob, shouting and fighting to get close to Ava. When she appeared at the plane door all hell let loose. It was suggested she leave by the cockpit door, but on turning to go, as explained by Hanna, someone yelled up to her in perfect English: 'Don't turn your ass on us, Ava.' She exploded! They managed to get her through to the small airport lounge, but she had been pinched and mauled every step of the way, and was soon on the verge of hysterics. On top of this she was booked into an old shabby hotel, not the Copacabana as was expected. Photographs showed Ava arriving, dishevelled and a broken shoe in hand. She was appalled at the hotel, and even more so when she learned that United Artists had agreed to that hotel in exchange for the management's paying the costs. After all, Ava Gardner staying there would have been good publicity for that hotel. Ava furiously threw her champagne glass to the floor and stormed out yelling: 'I can pay my own bills, and if United Artists can't pay theirs, it's too damned bad.' The press however told a wholly fantastic and fabricated story. The arriving drunk and disorderly, furniture being broken and the smashing of her glass were all believed as fact. The mêlée at the airport was not mentioned. These were the kind of stories the world wanted about Ava Gardner, and if papers and magazines could not get them, then one way or another they would just have to be fabricated.

Still, it was all good publicity for *Contessa*, and Metro did all right out of it too. Everywhere that Ava went in South America, Metro hauled out her old pictures and gave them an airing to capitalise on her visit. Billboards were plastered with her picture advertising Metro productions. But not a single member of MGM's South American management made any attempt to meet her: she was, after all, still on suspension.

The Barefoot Contessa opened in New York and later Los Angeles. Ava made a stunning appearance at both premières, and pictures of her in a slinky gown sped around the world. She was a knock-out.

But the film was not the unqualified success it had been hoped for. But although at the time it was compared unfavourably with Mankiewicz's *All About Eve*, along with *Eve*, now it is considered as his best work. The critics in America gave Ava a mixed appraisal. It was too slow for most American audiences and proved to be a bigger hit in Europe.

The film opened in Britain to fine reviews. All were ecstatic over Ava, 'One of Ava's best performances', 'It proves once and for all that Ava Gardner is the most glamorous star of the lot', and 'Humphrey Bogart shines –

but the big star is Ava'. Margaret Hinxman, who had taken over the reviews for *Picturegoer*, wrote:

> Every so often in this film someone observes that life isn't like a movie script. Certainly this screen life – the rise, decline and fall of a glamorous Spanish film star, couldn't be anything other than a movie script. But that couldn't matter less. It's the way director writer Mankiewicz has tricked the story out that makes it impressive – 'All about Eve-ish' dialogue, settings superb, brilliant acting performances. Ava Gardner – never more ravishing to look at – beautifully sustains this legend of a fascinating woman ... The film doesn't come off all along the line. But as a drama bursting at the seams with interesting things to see and hear, it's unusual.

The movie was described by everyone as intelligently written and directed, in many ways one of the year's best films. As in *Pandora*, Ava had been photographed by Jack Cardiff and looked absolutely stunning, and like *Pandora, Contessa* lingers on in the art-theatres.

Ava's feuding with Metro was finally resolved by a new contract, better pay, and more say in her films. Metro then announced that her next film would be their version of John Master's novel *Bhowani Junction*. As shooting was not due to start immediately, Ava went on another junket promoting *Contessa* around the world for United.

This tour took in Tokyo, Hong Kong, Singapore, Rome, Stockholm and Berlin, and everywhere she went, she caused a sensation. A Barefoot Contessa in the flesh was a sight to be seen: whether in Chinese-style dress in the orient or slinky gown in the west, Ava epitomised star glamour, possessing the style that many had thought gone for ever from the screen.

She flew straight from her tour to start work on *Bhowani Junction* in London, and then on to location in Pakistan.

Held in passionate embrace by Stewart Granger in a scene from Bhowani Junction, *1956*

John Master's book was a powerful work dealing with the partition of India. Ava would portray an Anglo-Indian girl, Victoria Jones. She really wanted to do this film, feeling that here at last was a role that had something to say and one that might prove she could act. Also she was looking forward to working with director George Cukor, who would admire her and become one of her few close friends. Cukor, it has been said, has a happy knack of getting the very best out of his female stars, and has been called a 'woman's director'. Ava worked diligently and happily under Cukor's expert direction, despite appalling conditions on location in Lahore, Pakistan. Being rather sensitive to the subject matter, India had refused permission to film there. The conditions were horrendous, living quarters were terrible and the food disgusting. Most of the crew suffered from severe illnesses, and only Ava seemed to take it all in her stride.

Cukor said of her: 'Ava was a gem, she was marvellously punctual and never complained even when it was clear the poor darling was exhausted. She was wonderful in the part.' The film's producer Pandro S. Berman recalled: 'I don't know how we got through it alive.'

Bhowani Junction emerged in 1956 as a well made and acted film, though slightly flawed by Metro's laundering of its content. The censor had cut several scenes, feeling that they were too provocative and, in the case of one passionate bedroom scene between Ava and Bill Travers, erotic. Ava came out of it all with credit. Her acting was excellent and *Junction* provided her with one of her most affecting performances – besides, no one ever looked as good in a sari as she did. The film was generally praised and was a big hit. *Picturegoer*'s review was typical:

In Hollywood jargon, this film has been a trouble film. A year of cutting and re-shooting preceded its showing . . . But, if this is trouble, let's have a lot more of it. The setting is post-war India just before the British withdrew,

Ava as Victoria Jones, Bhowani Junction, *1956*

and it's a hate-ridden, steamy India the screen has never had the initiative and the imagination to show before. It's a worthwhile film, despite dozens of faults. The central figure is an Anglo-Indian officer in the Women's Indian Army Corps (Ava), a girl with enough complexes to keep a psychiatrist happy for life. Deeply she feels her position, neither wholly British nor Indian. She tries to reconcile herself to marrying another touchy Anglo-Indian (Travers), but that won't work.

For a time she goes native, believing she can learn to love an Indian (Francis Matthews), but finally settles for the gruff British Colonel (Stewart Granger) who has been protecting her. This emotional dilly-dallying is given sharper urgency by the heated atmosphere of Indian politics. The plot disintegrates into messy pieces at the end. But location settings . . . with screaming crowd scenes and blood curdling violence – are magnificent.

The acting, too, is remarkable: from Ava's mixed-up anguish as the Anglo-Indian and Stewart Granger's plausible colonel to Freda Jackson's tight-as-a-ball portrayal of a fanatical Indian Communist.

After this Ava took off for Madrid, and announced that from now on Europe was home. She set about finding a house in her beloved Spain. From then on reports sifted from time to time into the world presses of various romances. Her affair with Dominguin had by now cooled to the stage of almost friendship. She had nursed the hopes that they would eventually marry, but he realised that she was not really in love with him. Besides, she was still married to Sinatra, and his influential Catholic family were opposed to the match. Both realised the situation could not carry on indefinitely, and they parted without rancour, remaining friends even after Dominguin had married Italian actress Lucia Bose.

She entered into an affair with Walter Chiari, whom she

had been dating occasionally for some years. He was an Italian comedian and described as Italy's Danny Kaye. This romance seemed at times to be very serious. Rumours of impending retirement were also rife. As Ava's desire for complete privacy grew so did the stories circulating about her. She refused to allow any interviews, which was resented by the newsmen. Deprived of stories because of her Garbo-like lifestyle, they invented. Fan magazines were particularly scurrilous. Articles appeared luridly titled: 'The strange fears of Ava Gardner', and 'Ava's private hell', and so on. When ever she did appear she was constantly hounded by photographers who contrived to take unflattering pictures of her. They were printed and headlined, 'She was beautiful once'. All this increased Ava's suspicious nature and hardened her protective shell.

From Madrid Metro sent her to Rome for *The Little Hut* (1957). She hated the script, but stated that it was the least

With David Niven in The Little Hut, *1957*

horrendous of all the scripts she had repeatedly turned down. It had started life as a very saucy French farce, concerning a man, his wife and his wife's lover, and the code for living worked out by them when all three are shipwrecked on a desert island.

This being 1957 the screen's strict censorship forced Metro to change much of the content, resulting in a considerably altered and whitewashed version of the original. It was further flawed by being filmed on the vast sound stages at Cinecitta, and not on location as it should have been. This made the film sound hollow and look artificial. The only consolation for Ava was that friends Stewart Granger, David Niven and beau Walter Chiari were in it. The film was not a big commercial success for MGM and they were furious when Ava told an interviewer that the film and her part were lousy. She told Hanna: 'I shouldn't have done it. The director was awful ... but what could I do? If I took another suspension, they would keep me at Metro the rest of my life.'

Picturegoer commented:

Frankly, the sight of a drenched human being emerging from the sea on to a sunny desert island shore is beginning to lose its piquancy on the screen. Even when the human being happens to be Ava Gardner looking terrific in something fancy knocked up by Dior. [The film is] based on a saucy French satire, but the spice got left out ... Married to a dullard English financier (Granger) whose resourcefulness stops short at romance, Ava whiles away her time with an old friend of the family (Niven) ... They find themselves castaways. The climate works wonders for Granger, who looks at his wife with a new light in his eyes. But, Niven, relegated to the 'little hut' especially built for him by Granger, feels himself the odd man out and suggests they should share Ava.

The threat of infidelity is talked about at great – and

sometimes witty – length. But no trespassing hand is laid on Ava. The usual desert island do-it-yourself situations are played out amusingly enough and the London scenes, that poke fun at British reserve and understatement, are as comically angled as a 'Punch' cartoon.

The three principals guy their characters with a gaily worldly air. But when, at the end, Ava assures hubby that 'nothing happened', she might have been giving a snap review of the picture.

With David Niven (left) and Stewart Granger in The Little Hut, *1957*

Ava, as seen through the eyes of caricaturist, Bois

As Lady Brett Ashley in The Sun Also Rises, *1957*

With *Hut* finished in Rome, Ava flew on to Monaco, for the fairytale wedding of Hollywood's Grace Kelly to Prince Rainier. Ava turned out to be one of the very few celebrities from the film capital to accept Grace's invitation. Most, reasoning that Grace would naturally get all the publicity, found reasons not to attend.

Ava then returned to Madrid and went to ground. But the newspapers were agog with excitement. Frank Sinatra was reporting to Madrid for work on the Stanley Kramer production *The Pride and the Passion*. It was even rumoured that Ava had been approached to play the role subsequently given to Sophia Loren. Much speculation was rife about there being a reconciliation between Ava and Frank. Technically they were still married because she had never picked up the divorce papers. It was reported that Frank had to pass Ava's villa every day on his way to the location, but there is no evidence that they ever met during his stay in Spain.

Ava felt she would like to do another Hemingway story, and thought seriously of asking MGM to purchase *A Farewell to Arms* from Paramount for her. She had always been successful as a Hemingway woman. The chance came, from 20th Century Fox, who offered her the part of Lady Brett Ashley, a beautiful hedonist and one of the lost generation between the wars, in their rendering of *The Sun Also Rises* (1957). The film was to be made entirely on location in Mexico, and was to be directed by Henry King who had also directed her in *Kilimanjaro*. Whilst in Mexico, Ava's marriage to Sinatra was finished officially, when she obtained a divorce.

She was none too pleased with the first draft of the *Sun* script by Peter Viertel, and took it along to Hemingway, whereupon, he declared he would sue the company if they proceeded with it as it was. A new scenario was therefore written to everyone's satisfaction. It all came across as a long, starry and very nearly great movie, and Papa Heming-

Rehearsing for The Sun Also Rises, *1957*

way described Ava as 'The most exciting woman of our generation'. She gave a performance that was sure and unerring and caught well the essential loneliness and haunted quality of Brett Ashley. Though to many she was just giving an extension of what was still believed to be her own character and lifestyle.

99

The film garnered excellent reviews and *Picturegoer*'s Margaret Hinxman was enthusiastic:

> If your first independent production 'Island in the Sun' was a lemon, Mr Zanuck, this one takes the sour taste away. Though Ernest Hemingway's novel isn't obvious filmable material – a desolate, drifting story about the aimless expatriates who congregated in Paris after the First World War – director Henry King and a top notch cast have welded it into a film of style, truth and haunting quality.
>
> Superficially, the photography catches brilliantly the effervescent glory of Paris, the crowded, sun-splashed richness of Spain, the grandiose grimness of the bullfights.
>
> A newspaper correspondent (Tyrone Power) is so severely wounded in the war that he's incapable of making love to a woman. The girl who loves him deeply (Ava) settles for any man to appease her hopeless longing for him. These are the main characters. In her flitting, ruinous progress, she ensnares a melancholy and obsessive writer (Mel Ferrer); a good time extrovert (Errol Flynn); and a boyish bullfighter (Robert Evans). But finally, this problem film ends with its problem intact.
>
> The playing is expert - from Power and Gardner. Mel Ferrer catches exactly the doomed loneliness of the writer who never quite fits in anywhere. There are two magnificently hilarious performances from Flynn (what a revelation) and Eddie Albert; and two important discoveries – Juliette Greco, as a wise boulevard slut; Robert Evans, the bullfighter. Hemingway, much screened and much mangled before, has never had it so good.

1959 saw Ava coming to the close of her Metro contract. Soon she would be an independent artiste. The need to make enough money to secure her future seemed overwhelming, and in a fit of bad judgement she accepted the

The Naked Maja, *1959*

role of the Duchess of Alba in *The Naked Maja*. Italian producer Goffredo Lombardo had long wanted to make a film about the painter Goya and his love for the Duchess of Alba. A merger between Titanus Productions and United Artists with distribution rights by MGM, and Ava's acceptance of the role made this possible. Metro tossed in $150,000 in return for the rights to every European country except Italy and a sizeable share of the profits. They stated that for Ava's services $350,000 was wanted, though she herself only got $90,000 of it for the film.

It was planned to film it in Madrid, which Ava was in full accord with. However, objections to the production were raised by the still-influential Alba family, and the filming was moved to Rome. There were troubles and delays from the start, mostly over the scripts. Ava herself had rejected quite a few. It seems the only good one had already been thrown out by the company, and that was by Ava's *Pandora* director, Albert Lewin.

'It's the same old story,' Ava retorted, 'If I take a suspension it means another year at Metro. Here I could be getting half a million dollars a picture like the others. Hell, that's probably what Metro gets for me anyhow.' Before *Maja* went into production, the European press was alive with reports and pictures of a bullfighting accident in which Ava was thrown from a startled horse, and then later, head covered in a blanket, hurrying furtively into London. The worst had happened, they said: 'the world's most beautiful animal' was horribly disfigured and would be scarred for life.

What had happened was that Ava, along with Chiari and some other friends, had gone to the ranch of Spanish bull-breeder Angelo Peralta. Since she was so fascinated by bullfighting, someone suggested she try her hand at the sport. It developed into a dare, and Ava accepted the challenge. Peralta put her on one of his finest horses, though she had little idea of how to ride, and she was given a special lance with which to bait the bull. The animal charged, and

Ava's horse reared, throwing her to the ground. Again the bull charged, this time at her, striking her cheek and throwing her into the air. Ava, crying hysterically, was carried into the ranch house. Her cheek began to swell, she had suffered a *hematoma*, a swelling caused by a blood clot forming on the inside of her cheek. She was frantic, and all of her old childhood fears of being scarred rushed to the surface. This fear originated from when, at the age of six, Ava had been accidentally hit under the eye with a hoe by her sister Myra. As the swelling increased, so did all of Ava's fears. The only thing she had, she felt, was her looks. Without them the career she so often said she despised would be finished. In the past she had remarked: 'I'm not afraid of death, I wear it on my bosom like a carnation. But I am afraid of being scarred.'

She flew into London to see Sir Archibald McIndoe, the famous plastic surgeon. He told her to leave it alone and it would go down of its own accord. She, only half reassured, flew next to New York for a second opinion, and was told that the swelling might be reduced by an injection. Ava contacted Sir Archibald again, who begged her not to let anyone touch it. She took his advice and returned to Madrid, where she sat out the time for it to heal. All the while in Hollywood the gossip was that she was deformed and would never appear in front of a camera again. It did heal, leaving no trace to the naked eye, only in Ava's mind. With all the rumours she had become increasingly nervy and the non-existent blemish had become magnified out of all proportion in her mind. She quarrelled constantly with Walter Chiari, and because someone at the accident had photographed it, and then released the pictures to the press, she accused Chiari of having engineered the whole thing.

Eventually filming on *Maja* began. Ava, still fretful, was absolutely in terror of going before a camera again. On top of this she did not get along with her co-star, the intense Anthony Franciosa. It was stated that the two stars hated each other. There were arguments over her cameraman and his efforts to dispel her haggard looks; the costumes were not right; and she refused to carry on filming unless it was filmed at night when the stifling sound stages would be cooler. Her only comment on the production to the *New York Times* was: 'The one decent thing about this job is that it's my last picture under the Metro contract. I'll be free in September.'

At last, with no help from Metro, Ava finished *Maja*. MGM's reluctance to help out in all the difficulties this film experienced had been due to the fact that it was a so-called stepchild production and no matter how poor the quality, they could not lose their investments. The film was awful, and though once again as the Duchess of Alba Ava at least looked magnificently beautiful, her performance was severely trounced. Ava it was conceded gave her worst performance and *Maja* failed to generate interest anywhere. Margaret Hinxman concluded;

As Mike Todd might have said: it ain't history, it ain't entertainment. But as a job of miscasting, it's highly spectacular. Maybe the opportunity to play the flamboyant Duchess of Alba satisfied Ava Gardner's yen for all things Spanish. But her stilted performance is hopelessly inadequate.

At least she conveys some affinity with the period – early nineteenth century. But, as the painter Goya, Anthony Franciosa looks and talks like a refugee from a Brooklyn pool-room.

None of this would have mattered so much if the film, admittedly handsome to look at, had had the adventurous zest of an old-fashioned period romance or dialogue that didn't sound like the balloons in a comic strip.

As it is, it tells a long, lingering tale of Goya's love affair with the Duchess, against a background of Spanish Court

With Anthony Franciosa in The Naked Maja, *1959*

intrigue, the Inquisition and dirty dealings with the dastardly invading French.

During this time Sinatra had made several trips to Europe. He contacted Ava while she was filming in Rome with a view to meeting. She agreed, but when he arrived in Rome she refused to see him or answer his calls. Later she did call to see him at his Rome hotel, where she gave him back his wedding ring, then left in tears. This gesture hurt Sinatra deeply, and Ava later regretted the impulse. Maybe the fact that he had been seeing a lot of a certain English beauty had motivated her.

With the disaster of *Maja* behind her Ava was now on her own. As a star, she was no longer under contract to Metro, though they tried to claim an extra three weeks because the studio said she had been ill that length of time during the shooting of *Bhowani Junction*. Both director George Cukor and co-star Stewart Granger disproved Metro's claim and the matter was quietly dropped. Without MGM to back her and protect her she had to start finding good film material for herself. Though she compared Metro to a slave camp, she was honest enough to admit to being scared without them. The most urgent need was to get decent films at a good percentage. Ava was determined to make a million quickly and then quit.

3

A GODDESS ALONE

STANLEY KRAMER, a respected director who usually tackled serious subjects, proposed making a screen version of the grim best seller by Neville Shute, *On the Beach* (1960). Nothing could be more serious than this movie, it dealt with a group of people in Australia awaiting the end of civilisation after a nuclear holocaust has wiped out the rest of the world. Kramer wanted Ava for the female lead, and it was the sort of part she needed as an independent artiste. The film, though off-beat, would be an important one and a winner for Ava.

Kramer contacted her and arranged a meeting and was slightly non-plussed when she failed to show up. When they did meet, he was impressed by her grasp of the character, though she seemed more interested in flamenco. Ava asked for $500,000 dollars but accepted $400,000, and set off for Australia where shooting was to be done.

Ava was completely professional while making the film and at first happy about working in Australia, a completely

On the set of On the Beach, *1960. Stanley Kramer, the producer and director, huddles beneath the camera*

Ava Gardner, Anthony Perkins and Donna Anderson in a scene from On the Beach, *1960*

new country to her. But soon the Australian press began circulating the same old stories as in Europe about her. Her complete immersion in the film was not what they expected from Gardner. Where were the romantic escapades? She was only once linked with an Australian tennis player during her stay. Where were the fireworks and tantrums? She did not supply these and the press were disappointed. They began sniping at her, and she, by now bored and restless at the locations, gave them fuel when she exclaimed: 'I'm here to make a film about the end of the world, and this sure is the place for it.' The Aussies just loved that remark!

Chiari had joined her on location in Melbourne, where she constantly quarrelled with him. He gradually came to realise that she did not love him as he loved her, and that

111

their affair was slowly coming to a close. Years later he would say of his relationship with her:

> For the most part, Ava and I were happy together. But I don't believe she ever totally and committedly loved me as I loved her. She was the most beautiful woman I had ever known. Yet somehow when we were together I often felt I was alone, that she had withdrawn from me in some mysterious and unsettling way, and that it was going to be impossible for me to fulfil her . . . I was enormously proud of her. But still I had the nagging feeling I could never possess her. The only one who 'possessed' Ava Gardner was that adorable Ava herself.

Walter Chiari had been her most devoted admirer through the years, following her around the world, catering to her capricious whims, often putting his own career at risk. But Ava had for too long felt that maybe he was trying to further his own career by his association with her. This was uncharitable of her for nothing was further from the truth. Later, she found out the extent of his devotion to her, but by then it was too late and Chiari would bow quietly out of her life.

Frank Sinatra turned up in Australia to give several concerts, maybe in response to Ava's plea. It was well known that they were together during his stay, and she did attend one of the concerts. But the press behaved exactly the same as in Europe and made it hell for them both. The film was finished and Ava hurried back to Madrid

On the Beach was well received by the public and a big commercial hit, as well as being critically acclaimed by most of the reviewers. Ava and Fred Astaire, uncharacteristically cast in a dramatic role, garnered the acting laurels and reaped the best reviews. All found her unglamourised portrayal a revelation. A few said that the role of a woman who had lived too hard was type-casting. The majority gave

Fred Astaire, Ava, Gregory Peck and Stanley Kramer, on the set of On the Beach, *1960*

her some of the best notices of her career. 'Miss Gardner has never looked worse or been more effective,' one reviewer concluded.

Of the film *Picturegoer* said:

This should have been the most controversial, vital and important film of the decade. Why isn't it? How can the spectacle of the civilized world dying in front of your eyes be so strangely unmoving? The subject is beyond politics and conventional discussion and there's no doubt that director (Kramer) feels deeply about it ... Because none of those characters is vitally alive or representative, one cannot become deeply concerned. For the film concentrates almost exclusively upon this small group. There is little feeling that other people outside their little, rather chi-chi world, are equally involved.

And surely not everyone would prepare to meet the end quite so nobly or unprotestingly. The treatment, too, is not only understated, but under dramatized. A frantic car race, in which the drivers deliberately attempt to crash and kill themselves, is the only dramatic extravagance.

A careful, admirable film, certainly. And particularly well acted by an attractively unglamourized Ava.

Professionally in the early sixties Ava seemed adrift and for her, as for so many middle-aged stars, the offers in an industry increasingly avid for youth were never very tempting. She accepted the role of a Spanish prostitute caught up in the Spanish Civil War and in love with a priest played by Dirk Bogarde. Another inadequate Anglo-Italian co-production financed by Metro, It was a total disaster, and got few bookings in the States and even less in Europe. The failure of *The Angel Wore Red* (1960) was disappointing, for both Ava and Dirk gave sincere and competent performances. The only reason Ava could have accepted such a role was her personal aim of making a million and then quitting.

Certainly the picture did her no good at all as an independent star. Though Dirk Bogarde said in an interview for the *Evening Standard* (1961):

It was a magnificent part for Ava. It would have done for her what 'Two Women' did for Sophia Loren. She really put her heart into it. I think she was anxious to be more selective and make better pictures. She played it without make-up, without a bra, with holes in her dress. Then the word came from Hollywood. This would not do. They wanted more glamour. They put a corset on her and tidied her up. The life went out of Ava after that. I was hoping that we could bank the money and then quietly forget it ever happened.

With Dirk Bogarde in The Angel Wore Red, *1960*

After this, Ava seemed reluctant to film again, and would not be seen on the screen for another three years. So her last venture must have made her as financially secure as she had wanted to be. It was stated that on the day she heard she had made her first million, she screamed with glee and yelled: 'Now I don't have to make any more fucking films.'

She spent her time restlessly travelling, going to the bullfights, and having flamenco parties that would last until dawn. Sleeping the day through and then repeating the partying. Dinner parties sometimes lasted as long as twenty-four hours. But Ava could soon become bored and would then retreat into her villa and virtually lose contact with the world. The image was changing from that of a playgirl into that of a beautiful but lonely woman seeking something in one capital after another. It was said that wherever she went a large pile of Sinatra records would go with her, and she would listen sadly to these through the night. Whether any of this was true was mere speculation, as Ava characteristically kept quiet. Nunnally Johnson, director of *Angel*, recalled the Ava of this period: 'She would cry a lot. She had no confidence in herself. She felt she couldn't act. She had no home, no base, no family. She missed them terribly. She felt she'd missed out on life. It was hard to believe her unhappiness.'

Philip Yordon said: 'Her manner had grown disdainful, bitter, superior, contemptuous,' and Stanley Kramer commented: 'Because she looks the way she does, everyone assumes Ava is sophisticated, intelligent and mature. In fact she is none of these things. She is a simple farm girl and she has the mind and mentality of a simple girl!'

When she did film again she agreed to work for Samuel Bronston in his made-in-Madrid movie *55 Days at Peking* (1963). Bronston had produced the spectacularly successful *El Cid*, and spent vast sums on the kind of films normally associated with Cecil B. de Mille. Most had been winners, but the end was in sight, the public had been surfeited with

Ava in 55 Days at Peking, *1963*

epic movies and the costs were becoming prohibitive. *Peking* cost four million and certainly looked it. Its stunning special effects were the real stars and the human element was swamped in all the grandeur. It was a big-star epic about the Boxer uprising in the city of the title. Ava played a Russian countess, romantically involved with Charlton Heston.

During its production much was made of Ava's behaviour, the cast and vast crowd scenes unnerved her and she was no longer the highly dedicated or disciplined performer she had been. From the outset, Heston had opposed her casting, and she his. But the European distributors insisted on her name on the film. Ava launched into a virulent attack on the script and her part from the moment she had signed on the dotted line. Maybe she was right, for it ended up with there never being a completed script. The principals found themselves being handed bits of paper before each day's shooting with that day's dialogue on it. Sometimes Heston and David Niven made it up as they went along.

This was unsettling for Ava who was in a highly strung state to begin with. Nicholas Ray had to handle her with kid gloves, and she never did really get along with him, or her co-stars. Most of the time she would lock herself in her dressing room and she mixed very little. As shooting progressed so she began arriving later and later on the set. Still neurotic about her now-undetectable facial blemish, she would storm off the set if she thought anyone was taking photographs of her, only to repeat the process on her return when she believed a group of extras were talking and laughing about her. She was fortifying herself before each take with a drink and this was playing havoc with her looks and humour.

Nicholas Ray suffered a heart attack and was unable to continue directing, so Guy Green was called in. With Green, Ava seemed to work well, and the suggestion that her troublesome behaviour caused the writers to kill her off halfway through the plot seems nonsense. In the finished

With Richard Burton in The Night of the Iguana, *1964*

film her demise comes just before the final Chinese on-slaught and the fade-out of the film. Philip Yordon who had worked on the script said of her: 'All through the picture she was constantly drunk ... She would remain in her dressing room, terrified by the thousands of extras, and her double appeared in endless over-the-shoulder shots. In many scenes ... Heston ... begged her to join him, she again hid, drank and sulked. The real reason was fear: she was terrified of the competition from the major British stars, David Niven and Dame Flora Robson.'

Most critics agreed that the film was gorgeous to look at, but thought Ava looked and acted tired. It failed at the box office which is surprising, for it did have a lot going for it:

spectacular sets – the recreation of the city of Peking was one of the largest sets ever built – beautiful period costumes in which Miss Gardner did look superb; and plenty of action. The story of the fifty-five days that the foreign legations held out against the hordes of Imperial China was well made and a sweeping adventure yarn with, thankfully, not a Roman toga or legion in sight. Its failure certainly helped Bronston on the road to bankruptcy.

Ava was next scheduled to play in *The Pink Panther* (1964). But the demands she made were so great that the company dropped her. Peter Ustinov had been cast as Inspector Clouseau, but after Ava was dropped he also bowed out. It was eventually made with Robert Wagner, David Niven, Capucine and Claudia Cardinale, and the inspired casting of Peter Sellers as Clouseau.

Her next two film ventures would do much to redress the failure of her last two. For Paramount she took on a small but pivotal role in an extremely good story on the theme: could the army take over the government of the USA? In John Frankenheimer's *Seven Days in May* (1964), Ava played Eleanor Holbrook, the cast-off mistress of General Scott (Burt Lancaster) who is involved in a plot to overthrow the US government. Colonel Casey (Kirk Douglas) is called in to foil the plans. He uses Ava to obtain some incriminating love letters to her from Scott. Despite the brevity of her part – just three scenes – she did very well in this film, and showed that she really understood that woman, saddened by her experiences of life and men. This time she received universal praise. Bosley Crowther (*New York Times*) who had, throughout her career, been her severest critic at last conceded that she was 'superb'. Ava liked the film, feeling that here at last was a motion picture of merit. But was terribly upset by her aged apearance on the screen. John Frankenheimer recalled that she was never punctual during filming and was still drinking heavily, but he was more than pleased with her approach to the part.

Next John Huston persuaded her into his forthcoming production of Tennessee Williams' play *The Night of the Iguana* (1964). She took some persuading: she had great self doubts about accepting the part of the sexy and earthy hotel keeper, especially as it had been played on the stage by Bette Davis and Shelley Winters, and Davis was after the screen role. She was also terrified of working with the high-powered cast Huston had assembled, Richard Burton, Deborah Kerr and young Sue Lyon of *Lolita* fame. Huston prevailed and gladly she trusted him enough to accept, though having once signed, her doubts returned and she tried to get out of it. Huston said of her: 'She was – is – a very fine actress, though she thinks she's lousy. I knew she had the kind of random, gallant, wild, openness Maxine had along with "the other side" of Ava, which is very "close" and almost secretive.' Ava went on to give a performance that was magnificent, as was the film. It is probably the best version of a Williams play transferred to the screen.

It was filmed at a small Mexican place called Puerto Vallarta, at that time almost inaccessible by land, so all personnel and equipment had to be brought in by boat. Somehow the press managed to turn up in droves. The main attraction was not only the cast but the relationships between them. Ava had at one time dated Peter Viertel who was accompanying wife Deborah Kerr, and Burton was then at the height of his *Cleopatra* affair with Elizabeth Taylor. Much excitement was aroused from the fact that Miss Taylor followed Burton to Mexico, most days sitting on the sidelines watching her man, keeping him from Ava's preda-tory clutches, no doubt! They all seemed to feel sure that Burton and Gardner would make a play for each other, but they were sadly mistaken. All acted in a thoroughly pro-fessional manner and worked hard at making a very worthwhile film, although Ava did remark that Burton was the type of man she should have married.

John Huston gave each of them a gold-plated derringer

With Deborah Kerr and Richard Burton, rehearsing a scene for
The Night of the Iguana, *1964*

with gold bullets inscribed with the names of the others. Deborah Kerr remarked: 'I sensed a certain nervousness in the laughter and thanks,' and Huston told them they could use the guns should the competition become too fierce.

Iguana was highly thought of critically and justly deserved all the acclaim it received. Ava garnered some of the best notices of her career.

Bosley Crowther said: 'appropriate . . . is Ava Gardner as the owner and mistress of the hotel, which she personally imbues with a raucous and blowzy decadence. Her loose-jointed sweeps across the premises, her howling gibes at the clattering guests, and her free deportment with a couple of glistening beach boys does help to steam the atmosphere.'

Above: The Night of the Iguana, *1964*

Opposite page: Ava, as she appeared in The Bible, *1966*

With Catherine Deneuve in Mayerling, *1970*

Ava did not film again until 1966, and again it was for Huston, by now a warm friend and favoured director. For him, she played the small role of Sarah, wife to Abraham in his truly lengthy undertaking of *The Bible*. Ava managed to give a sincere and moving performance and did bring some dignity to the rather boring second half of the film. The film, slow and stately, was generally deplored by the critics, but became a box-office success.

After *Bible* Ava was seen in the company of her co-star George C. Scott. He was absolutely crazy about her, but it is doubtful that she was in love with him. Scott followed her to London, but the romance broke up after a row when he was thrown out of London's Savoy hotel after breaking up some furniture in his suite, battering Ava's door down and roughing her up. She had to escape his attentions by fleeing the hotel through the kitchens. For despite all the stories of hellraising on her part, Ava was embarrassed by the incident. Scott it seems trailed her to Los Angeles and repeated the assault. Eventually he went into a nursing home.

Shortly after that she left Spain for good, her love affair with that country had faded and she settled in London, where she now lives quietly in an exquisitely furnished apartment near Hyde Park. She moved there so discreetly that most people never even realised that one of the world's most beautiful women had settled in their midst.

She then took on the role of Omar Sharif's mother, the Empress Elizabeth of Austria, in Terence Young's reworking of the classic Charles Boyer success *Mayerling*. Sharif was the Crown Prince, and many said Ava was miscast. She should surely have played one of his mistresses at least. But the part of Maria Vetsera, his young mistress, went to Catherine Deneuve, whose appearance seemed insipid alongside Ava. Deneuve proved that there was not a single actress around who could generate the kind of excitement and glamour that Gardner could. Only James Mason as the

Emperor Franz Joseph received good reviews. Ava's cameo role was hardly mentioned, yet she and Mason acted well together, and she movingly brought to life the essential sadness, loneliness and restlessness of Elizabeth. The period clothes of the 1880s made her look surpassingly beautiful. Ultimately *Mayerling*, over-long and romantic, was a flop. It might have done better business if they had chucked out the parts played by Sharif and Deneuve and concentrated on Ava and Mason as the tragic Emperor and Empress of Austria.

As the permissive seventies rolled in, film roles for mature stars were hard to come by. Ava turned down many scripts that reflected the new climate, and absolutely refused to take on anything that required her to strip. 'I made it as a star dressed, if I haven't got it dressed, I don't want it,' she said.

There were plans for her to co-star with Lana Turner in a thriller, but they came to nothing. Maybe because her career never meant that much to her, Ava never resorted to the horror movie in an attempt to keep her name in the forefront, as so many of her contempories had. There is no sadder sight than a once great name playing second fiddle to a monster.

Roddy McDowall then asked her to star in his made-in-Britain project *Tam-Lin* (1970). Ava, out of friendship for McDowall, agreed. She found herself playing Michaela Cazaret, an extremely wealthy but ageing widow, surrounded by a group of young people who keep her amused. After her young lover leaves her for another, she uses every means including witchcraft to hang on to her looks and exact her revenge. She enjoyed making it and being directed by former child actor McDowall, and was bitter when the film was shelved for two years. It had gone into production under the banner of Commonwealth United and ran into problems, not least being the continued interference from the studio and the eventual collapse of Commonwealth. The

The Life and Times of Judge Roy Bean, *1972*

film was later acquired by American International for distribution, but it was so cut about that it was hardly recognisable to McDowall. The title got changed several times, starting out as *Toys* and finally being known as both *Tam-Lin* and *The Devil's Widow*. It was finally released in the States in 1972, had few bookings and was quickly sold to television.

Ava then made her first trip to Hollywood to film in years. She did a cameo role for John Huston in his 1972 western *The Life and Times of Judge Roy Bean*. Paul Newman played Bean, the lawman, and Ava the British music hall star and beauty, Lily Langtry. Roy Bean has a lifelong passion for Miss Langtry and loves her through collecting every available portrait of her and carrying on a correspondence. Ava's part was very brief, appearing in only the last five minutes or so after Bean's death. It required her services for just three days. She said she accepted the part because every winter she likes to holiday in Acapulco for water skiing, and felt that the film company might as well pay for it. Huston paid her $50,000.

A train pulls into a deserted town called Langtry, the camera moves in on the train. She sits at the window of a carriage in full close up, swathed in pink. Suddenly the face lights up into a smile, and wham! The legendary beauty of Ava Gardner knocks you for six. Time has moved on for Ava, but her beauty has grown. Gone, naturally, is the dewy splendour of her early Hollywood days. In its place is the mature grandeur of a woman who has lived life to the full. But where once there had been turbulence now there is serenity. Thus one sees Ava in one of her all-too-rare screen appearances. After the film for Huston, Ava seemed to pick up the threads of her career, and several films followed, all of varying quality.

Earthquake (1974) proved to be a blockbuster of a disaster movie and became one of Hollywood's all time grossers. For its stunning special effects it won several awards: indeed

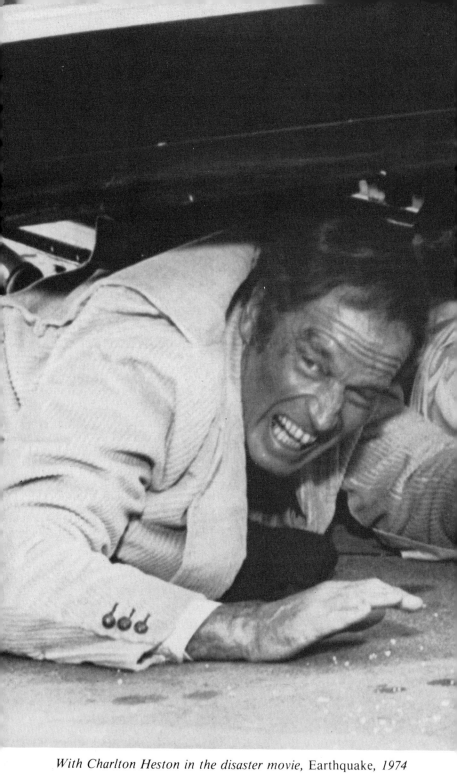

With Charlton Heston in the disaster movie, Earthquake, *1974*

these effects were the real stars of the picture. Once the Los Angeles earthquake got under way the actors just could not compete. Ava co-starred again with Charlton Heston, playing his wife and loathing his mistress, with whom she finds herself trapped below ground. This time she got along with Heston as well as Mark Robson, whom she had not liked on *The Little Hut*. The turbulent Ava of old seemed a thing of the past; she drank more sparingly, and was rarely seen on the Hollywood scene. Of her film role she told a reporter: 'Charlton Heston and I play a scene in a raging torrent. At one point the water actually ripped off the wig I was wearing. It was realistic enough. God knows I felt bruises for a week. But I don't think you could call that acting. No, I'm not an actress.'

Ava's next three films were all made in Europe. *Permission to Kill* (1976) went into production around Vienna, in fact the locations were the best part of the movie. It was an overly talkative spy melodrama with very little action. Ava and Dirk Bogarde fared none too well in this one, he as an intelligence agent bent on getting political exile Bekim Fehmiu assassinated, and Ava as Fehmiu's ex-mistress who gets drawn into the plot. The film was generally considered trite and boring, and was not likely to add any lustre to its participants' careers. *Films and Filming* commented: 'we are conscious of Miss Gardner's filmic intelligence from previous and happier occasions' which suitably sums up the feeling one would get from several of her film roles that followed.

The mightily expensive American-Russian co-production of Maurice Maeterlinck's 1908 fairy story about two children searching for the *Bluebird of Happiness* is the story of a production that went wrong. It boasted a strong cast with Ava playing Luxury, Elizabeth Taylor in the lead, Jane Fonda and Cicely Tyson and a strong back up of British stalwarts. Most of the trouble lay in Russia. When the company moved to Leningrad to start filming, they found

(From left to right) Roddy McDowall, Myrna Loy, George Cukor and Ava celebrate at a reception held in Mr Cukor's honour

that the Russians just had not got any up-to-date filming equipment. So most of the gear had to be imported from the States. On top of this the Russian crew were unused to working with the sophisticated colour stock, and then refused to work overtime. The food made most of the American and English crews ill, so more supplies had to be flown in from London. There continued to be delays and illnesses, and at one stage it looked as if the whole production would close down – especially after the Kirov Ballet withdrew from the picture. George Cukor, the film's director, managed to put it together from this shambles, though the Russians still worked too slowly for their western counterparts. Eventually it ran over the budget to the cost of eight million dollars.

Ava worked well with Cukor whom she both loved and respected, although her shyness would occasionally manifest itself, and on those occasions she would lock herself in her dressing room. For a while the film was shelved, but it finally reached the American screens in 1976. Few enthused over it and it quickly vanished. So far it has not been shown on any cinema screens in the west. In Russia it was said that it was a mighty hit. It did make a belated appearance on British television for the Easter break in 1981. It was part of a short season of George Cukor films and was declared a disaster, certainly not one of the distinguished director's finer efforts.

Ava next guested in the Sir Lew Grade-Carlo Ponti co-production of *The Cassandra Crossing* (1977), starring Sophia Loren and Richard Harris, with guest stars Ava, Burt Lancaster, Ingrid Thulin and Martin Sheen. The plot concerned the fate of a group of passengers exposed to a deadly virus brought aboard a Geneva-to-Stockholm express by a young terrorist. The authorities place the express and its passengers into quarantine, and since no country will accept them the train is diverted to the bridge of the title. A crossing that may or may not still be there. The climax of the film, a mixture of thriller and disaster movie, is a spectacular train crash. Ava, as the wife of a German millionaire arms dealer on board with her young lover, came off fairly well in this. She was smartly gowned and had some amusing lines. But somehow, it was not to become a big success. Later Ava was to find herself, along with star Richard Harris, Carlo Ponti and wife Sophia Loren, arraigned by the Italian courts. All were accused of spiriting art treasures out of Italy during the filming of *The Cassandra Crossing*. Both Harris and Ava faced immediate arrest should they set foot on Italian soil. Eventually the case was not proven and was dropped. The Pontis, however, would continue to battle

Permission to Kill, *1976*

With Elizabeth Taylor in The Bluebird, *1976*

with courts over tax for several more years.

Ava then went to New York for location shooting on Michael Winner's *The Sentinel* (1977) in which she was cast as a mysterious house agent who leases an apartment to Cristina Raines in a large, gloomy and otherwise empty house. Strange things keep occurring to Miss Raines and ultimately the house is revealed as the centre for occult horrors. Miss Raines finds herself drawn into devil worship and more besides. Ava's part was small, just three scenes, but she still retained much of her old allure. The film was spoilt by a rather silly ending and, in the vein of the popular vogue for films dealing with the devil, was a disappointment. The critics lambasted it, but it did manage to earn back its costs.

On these trips to the States, usually once a year, Ava would stay with sister Bappie in her unpretentious house in Hollywood. She seldom went out on the town on these visits, but did attend the odd première such as MGM's *That's Entertainment*, and a special tribute to George Cukor.

1980 found Ava playing an alcoholic television personality in another disaster movie, *City on Fire*. Her companions in terror were Henry Fonda, Susan Clark and Shelley Winters. This film has not met with great success and after a couple of weeks at a London cinema, this fire obviously failed to ignite and it vanished from public showing.

Then it was a very brief appearance as the wife of an American senator in a rather good political thriller called *The Kidnapping of the President*. Ava's last screen appearance to date was as a patroness to the author D. H. Lawrence in an excellent film tracing the journeyings of Lawrence in Europe and Mexico. Ian McKellan portrayed the writer, and others in the distinguished cast were Janet Suzman and Penelope Keith. *The Priest of Love* (1982) received much critical praise and both McKellan and Ava are in line for awards.

So in 1982, this legendary beauty is still considered an

With Cristina Raines in The Sentinel, *1977*

important enough name for cameo roles. That the parts are smaller is probably as much Ava's choice as for any other reason, as she has always maintained her dislike of filming and will only work when she wants to.

On her career Ava told the *Ladies' Home Journal*:

Being a film star is still a big damn bore. I do it for the money, that's all. After all these years I don't know a damn thing about movies. I was put under contract when I was eighteen because I was pretty, and since I made my

first picture I haven't done a damn thing that's worthwhile
... I've often tried to give it up. But I've got to do
something and I don't know how to do anything else ... If
I had more drive, more interest, maybe I'd have done
better; I don't know. As it is I never know what's going
on. As for acting, I know nothing about it.

In 1966 she told Rex Reed, a New York columnist:

What did I ever do worth talking about? Everytime I tried
to act they stepped on me. That's why it's such a goddam
shame. I've been a movie star for twenty-five years and
I've got nothing, nothing to show for it ... But I never
brought anything to this business and I have no respect for
acting. Maybe if I had learned something it would be
different. But I never did anything to be proud of. Out of
all those movies, what can I claim to have done?

Two titles were mentioned by Reed. 'Hell, baby, after
twenty-five years in this business if all you've got to show for
it is *Mogambo* and *The Hucksters* you might as well give up'.
She hasn't, and for that one can be glad.

She is by no means a great actress but she is a fine and
sensitive one, even though the majority of her film roles
never stretched her talents to the limit. She has managed,
admirably, with her great screen presence to endow many a
cardboard character with genuine warmth, vitality and life,
and in her later career, when the appearances grew rarer,
she still generated her own brand of sexuality and excitement, and quite a few films have been enlivened by the
Gardner charisma. There are parts one would have liked to
have seen Ava in, parts she could have played magnificently,
given the chance and a sympathetic director. Roles such as
those played by Garbo, whom Ava resembles, not only in
beauty but in her constant shunning of publicity.

Ava's qualities were right for *Anna Karenina*, and one would have relished her as Hedda Gabler, or, had she the training, as Lady Macbeth. She could have been a stunning Cleopatra, especially in the tragic mausoleum scene from Shakespeare's play. That none of these roles were brought to life by her is our loss. However, what she has left us is more than enough. A standard Metro starlet emerged as a player of intelligence, sincerity and of course great beauty, and certainly did not warrant her remark: 'Everytime I tried to act, really tried, they slammed me.'

The Ava of today leads a quiet life in London, far removed from the turbulent and hectic star years, when a female reporter could write of her: 'She was her customary self, as amiable as an adder. She gave a look Medusa might have envied. Elizabeth Taylor and Ava are as spoiled as medieval queens. They expect men to fall at their feet, and they are accustomed to being catered to and having everything done for them.'

In those years the insecurity Ava felt about herself and her career made the harsher side of her nature assert itself. She was erratic, constantly spurning friends. Her nocturnal phone calls were notorious and not to answer them was taken as a deliberate snub by Ava. Once her natural warmth and humour returned she could woo the bewildered friend back by the complete sincerity of her apologies. Director Nunnally Johnson recalled:

She was a real headache for a production company. She travelled with thirty pieces of luggage, all of which had to go with the plane as she was terrified of losing it. She was a sultana in terms of her accommodations, the accoutrements of a star. She had a succession of secretaries who collapsed under the strain of handling all of these things. Sometimes a man, sometimes a woman. They couldn't take the pace. She had to be escorted to nightclubs, she couldn't go alone ... She'd stay up all night.

143

The constant stories about supposed feuds and fights with those around her increased her ill humour. She was said to have had a terrible fight with Shelley Winters over Anthony Franciosa in a Rome nightclub; attacked a girl with a broken bottle; smashed up photographers' cameras. She would keep everyone of her intimates on the hop, catering to her every whim. Ava would quibble over the smallest detail and appear terribly mean, money-wise, and in the next breath would shower those she loved with just about everything they could wish for.

So much was also made of the drinking bouts that Ava herself has talked on rare occasions about it: 'I drink only for the effect, I can't ever remember enjoying a drink. The only reason I do it is to get over my shyness,' and 'I'm not the great big boozer the press makes me out to be. I'm really rather a sneaky drinker. I'll pretend I have a lot more than I actually have ... I love parties and staying up late, but I believe that nothing must interfere with your work. If you can't get out of bed the next morning, or go straight from the party to work, then you should knock it off.'

But of course all the stories circulating at this period were just what the fans and press wished to believe, and the remark, 'There goes Ava, leaving nothing behind and nothing to look forward to', summed it all up.

That is all behind her. On rare occasions some cameraman will get a shot of this ex-goddess of the cinema, exercising her dog in Hyde Park or at a Wimbledon tennis tournament, a picture has appeared, but it is a rare occurrence. On her decision to live in England she told reporters: 'I have always loved England ... London, they take three or four photographs when you arrive and then they forget you exist. I love London, the climate, the people. I love the rain in London. The thin, fine rain ... it gives me tranquillity for a time. It appeases me,' and again, 'I like to live simply and out of the public eye. I can do these things in England. I am left alone. My friends and I have dinner at our homes or go to parties in public places without being disturbed. That isn't too much to ask.' So seemingly she has found the lifestyle she craved here. She is independent and can take off for any part of the world on a whim. In London she is left alone and – like Garbo – this is what she has always wanted.

Today's Ava has a close regard for her ex-husbands and says: 'I like them all. I have love and affection for the men I married. My husbands are all good chums, even though the marriages did not work. The funny thing is that, in spite of three divorces, I was a pretty good wife. That's what I'm good at really ... looking after a man and cooking his dinner.' She seldom mentions Mickey Rooney, but provided him with financial help when he hit hard times, and was furious with Metro, saying: 'Mickey made a fortune for Metro, but when he was through and needed their help, they tossed him right out on his can.'

'When I met Artie Shaw I was twenty, but I told him I was only nineteen. And you know why? Because I have never had any higher schooling and was ashamed of my ignorance. I hoped he'd accept me if he thought I was one year younger.'

It is obvious that Sinatra is still the one man that she thinks of with the most affection. They remain friends, and she is pleased that he has happily married, and even now they meet from time to time. She was upset when Nancy Sinatra Jnr, writing a book on her father, requested information from her 'from all those who have had close contact with him'. Ava's hurt remark to that was, 'Close contact? Doesn't she remember I married him?'

On the failures of her marriages and romances she has mused: 'I have an affinity for jerks. But that won't stop me looking for the right man. Every time I fall in love, or think I'm in love, I'll get married. I will try and make the best of my marriage, but I think I'll die if another marriage fails. And if I don't die, I'll kill myself.' John Huston said, 'She's become tired of passion ... She loved one man at a time, she was never promiscuous. Three husbands and maybe six lovers – that's a remarkable record for a woman of her beauty and fame and attraction.' Ava was quoted as saying: 'People say Liz (Taylor) and I are unfaithful, but we aren't saints, we do not hide our loves hypocritically, and when we love we are loyal and faithful to our men.' Since her move to London from Spain there has been no serious liaison with anyone, at least none that has ever come to the public's notice. A few years back Ava remarked, 'That's what I really miss, not love, but cuddles!'

So the 1980s find a woman alone, living her life of retreat in her quiet, green oasis. Those who do catch a glimpse of her report that she is still as stylish as ever, she dresses simply but with taste, a woman of great and abiding beauty. Ava has said, 'I don't mind growing old. I'd like to live to be 150 . . . I'll even have a fellow then. If I have to go before my time, this is how I'll go – cigarette in one hand, glass of scotch in the other.' On her looks she has commented: 'What are looks? Oh it's nice to be told you're pretty, but there are more important things. They used to go on about how beautiful I was as a young girl, but I much prefer the way I look now. I was so darned uninteresting then. There comes a time when you've simply got to face the fact that you're an old broad. And I have.'

As this still-lovely lady approaches her sixties, another remark of hers fits. 'I'm not scared of growing old. Not at all. I'll never be one of those women who look in mirrors and weep. I don't lie about my age. What's the point? It's in the reference books if anyone wants to check.'

Throughout her career younger actresses definitely found her awe-inspiring, and one such admirer exclaimed after a meeting, 'It wasn't an introduction but an event.' She was beloved by photographers who always claimed, 'She's a delight to shoot. She has no flaws.' Elizabeth Taylor was given to saying that she considered Ava was the most beautiful woman in the world. In her early days at Metro, an executive burst in on her in her dressing room. She was naked from the waist up, he was told off in no uncertain terms in language that wouldn't disgrace a navvie. But he later said that in all his life he had never seen anything so beautiful.

Britain's Roland Culver, who appeared with her in *Singapore* back in 1947, recollected in an article on the screen goddesses he had worked with: 'I adored this woman, she was the most beautiful of the lot.'

For a woman who honestly believed she had no talent whatsoever, Ava Gardner is still one of the great stars of the cinema, and one of the legendary women of our time.

FILMOGRAPHY

Ava's first reported screen appearance was in *We Were Dancing* (1942). In all her subsequent pictures up to 1944, her appearances were little more than as an extra. The films were:

1942: *We Were Dancing; Joe Smith American; Sunday Punch; Calling Dr Gillespie; This Time for Keeps; Kid Glove Killer; Pilot No 5.*

1943: *Hitler's Madman; Reunion in France; Du Barry was a Lady; Young Ideas; Lost Angel; Ghosts on the Loose* (Monogram Pictures).

1944: *Swing Fever; Music for Millions.*

All Metro Goldwyn Mayer productions except *Ghosts on the Loose.*

THREE MEN IN WHITE

MGM, 1944, black and white

Director: Willis Goldbeck
Screenplay: Martin Berkeley, Harry Ruskin
Based on characters created by Max Brand
Photography: Ray June
Music: Nathaniel Shilkret
Running time: 85 minutes

PRINCIPAL CAST

Lionel Barrymore:	Dr Leonard Gillespie
Van Johnson:	Dr Randall Adams
Key Luke:	Dr Lee Wong How
Marilyn Maxwell:	Ruth Edley
Ava Gardner:	Jean Brown

MAISIE GOES TO RENO

MGM, 1944, black and white

Producer: George Haight
Director: Harry Beaumont
Screenplay: Mary McCall Jr
Based on characters by Wilson Collison
Photography: Robert Planck
Music: David Snell
Running time: 90 minutes

PRINCIPAL CAST

Ann Sothern:	Maisie Ravier
John Hodiak:	Flip Hanahan
Tom Drake:	Bill Fullerton
Marta Lindon:	Winifred Ashbourne
Paul Cavanagh:	Pelham
Ava Gardner:	Gloria Fullerton

151

SHE WENT TO THE RACES

MGM, 1945, black and white, release date: 21 January 1946

Producer: Frederick Stephani
Director: Willis Goldbeck
Screenplay: Lawrence Hazard
Photography: Charles Salerno
Music: Nathaniel Shilkret
Running time: 86 minutes

PRINCIPAL CAST

James Craig:	Steve Canfield
Frances Gifford:	Dr Ann Wotters
Ava Gardner:	Hilda Spotts
Edmund Gwenn:	Dr Pecke

WHISTLE STOP

United Artists, 1946, black and white, release date: 6 May, 1946

Producer: Seymour Nebenzal
Director: Leonide Moguy
Screenplay: Philip Yordon
Photography: Russell Metty
Music: Nathaniel Shilkret
Running time: 85 minutes

PRINCIPAL CAST

George Raft:	Kenny
Ava Gardner:	Mary
Victor McLaglen:	Gillo
Tom Conway:	Lew Lentz

The Killers

THE KILLERS

Universal International, 1946, black and white, release date: 13 January 1946

Producer: Mark Hellinger
Director: Robert Siodmak
Screenplay: Anthony Veiller, John Huston
From a story by Ernest Hemingway
Photography: D. S. Horsley, Woody Bredell
Music: Miklos Rosza
Running time: 105 minutes

PRINCIPAL CAST

Burt Lancaster:	Swede
Ava Gardner:	Kitty Collins
Edmond O'Brien:	Reardon
Albert Dekker:	Colfax

THE HUCKSTERS

MGM, 1947, black and white, release date: 4 August 1947

Producer: Arthur Hornblower, Jr
Director: Jack Conway
Screenplay: Luther Davis
From a novel by Frederick Wakeman
Photography: Harrold Rossen
Music: Lennie Hayton
Running time: 115 minutes

PRINCIPAL CAST

Clark Gable:	Victor Albee Norman
Deborah Kerr:	Kay Dorrance
Sydney Greenstreet:	Evan Llewellyn Evans
Adolphe Menjou:	Mr Kimberley
Ava Gardner:	Jean Ogilvie
Keenan Wynn:	Buddy Hare

154

Singapore

SINGAPORE

Universal International, 1947, black and white, release date: 5 January 1948

Producer: Jerry Bresler
Director: John Brahm
Screenplay: Seton I. Miller
Photography: Maury Gertsman
Music: Daniel Amfitheatrof
Running time: 79 minutes

PRINCIPAL CAST

Fred MacMurray: Matt Gordon
Ava Gardner: Linda
Roland Culver: Michael Van Leydon
Thomas Gomez: Mr Mauribus
Richard Haydon: Chief Inspector Hewitt
Spring Byington: Mrs Bellows

ONE TOUCH OF VENUS

Universal International, 1948, black and white

Producer: Lester Cowan
Director: William A. Seiter
Screenplay: Harry Kurnitz, Frank Tashlin
Based on the musical play
Photography: Franz Planer
Music: Kurt Weill, Ogden Nash
Running time: 82 minutes

PRINCIPAL CAST

Robert Walker: Eddie Hatch
Ava Gardner: Venus/Venus Jones
Dick Haymes: Joe
Eve Arden: Molly Grant
Olga San Juan: Gloria
Tom Conway: Whitfield Savorny

The Bribe

THE BRIBE

MGM, 1949, black and white, release date: 27 June 1949

Producer: Pandro S. Berman
Director: Robert Z. Leonard
Screenplay: Marguerite Roberts
Based on a story by Frederick Nebel
Photography: Joseph Ruttenberg
Music: Miklos Rozsa
Running time: 98 minutes

PRINCIPAL CAST

Robert Taylor:	Rigby
Ava Gardner:	Elizabeth Hinton
Charles Laughton:	A. J. Bealer
Vincent Price:	Carwood
John Hodiak:	Tug Hinton

THE GREAT SINNER

MGM, 1949, black and white, release date: 12 December 194

Producer: Gottfried Reinhardt
Director: Robert Siodmak
Screenplay: Christopher Isherwood
From the novel by Fyodor Dostoevsky
Photography: George Folsey
Music: Bronislau Kaper
Running time: 110 minutes

PRINCIPAL CAST

Gregory Peck:	Fyodor Dostoevsky
Ava Gardner:	Pauline Ostrovski
Melvyn Douglas:	Armand De Glasse
Walter Huston:	General Ostrovski
Ethel Barrymore:	Granny
Frank Morgan:	Aristide Pitard
Agnes Moorehead:	Emma Getzel

The Great Sinner

EAST SIDE, WEST SIDE

MGM, 1949, black and white, release date: 19 June 1950

Producer: Voldemare Vetliguin
Director: Mervyn Leroy
Screenplay: Isobel Lennart
From the novel by Marcia Davenport
Photography: Charles Rosher
Music: Miklos Rozsa
Running time: 108 minutes

PRINCIPAL CAST

Barbara Stanwyck:	Jessie Bourne
James Mason:	Brandon Bourne
Van Heflin:	Mark Dwyer
Ava Gardner:	Isabel Lorrisan
Cyd Charisse:	Rosa Senta
Nancy Davis:	Helen Lee
Gale Sondergaard:	Nora Kernan

MY FORBIDDEN PAST (Carriage Entrance)

RKO, 1951, black and white, release date: 9 July 1951

Producer: Robert Sparks, Polan Banks
Director: Robert Stevenson
Screenplay: Marion Parsonette
Photography: Harry J. Wild
Music: Frederick Hollander
Running time: 81 minutes

PRINCIPAL CAST

Robert Mitchum:	Dr Mark Lucas
Ava Gardner:	Barbara Beaurevel
Melvyn Douglas:	Paul Beaurevel
Lucile Watson:	Aunt Eula
Janis Carter:	Corinne

PANDORA AND THE FLYING DUTCHMAN

British Lion – Romulus, MGM, 1951, colour, release date: 5 March 1951

Producer: Albert Lewin, Joseph Kaufman
Director: Albert Lewin
Screenplay: Albert Lewin
Photography: Jack Cardiff
Music: Alan Rawstherne
Running time: 123 minutes

PRINCIPAL CAST

James Mason:	Hendrik Van Der Zee
Ava Gardner:	Pandora Reynolds
Nigel Patrick:	Stephen Cameron
Sheila Sim:	Janet
Harold Warrender:	Geoffrey Fielding
Mario Cabre:	Juan Montalvo
Marius Goring:	Reggie Demarest

SHOWBOAT

MGM, 1951, colour, release date: 24 September 1951

Producer: Arthur Freed
Director: George Sidney
Screenplay: John Lee Mahin
Music: Jerome Kern and Oscar Hammerstein II
Photography: Charles Rosher
Running time: 108 minutes

PRINCIPAL CAST

Kathryn Grayson:	Magnolia Hawks
Ava Gardner:	Julie Laverne
Howard Keel:	Gaylord Ravenal
Joe E. Brown:	Captain Andy Hawks
Robert Sterling:	Stephen Baker
Agnes Moorehead:	Parthy Hawks
Marge Champion:	Ellie May Shipley
Gower Champion:	Frank Schultz
William Warfield:	Joe
Leif Erickson:	Pete

LONE STAR

MGM, 1952, black and white, release date: 10 March 1952

Producer: Z. Wayne Griffith
Director: Vincent Sherman
Screenplay: Borden Chase
*Photography:*Harold Rossen
Music: David Buttolph
Running time: 94 minutes

PRINCIPAL CAST

Clark Gable:	Devereaux Burke
Ava Gardner:	Martha Ronda
Broderick Crawford:	Thomas Craden
Lionel Barrymore:	Andrew Jackson
Beulah Bondi	Minniver Bryan

One man's restless search for adventure—and love.
Three women's desperate attempts to share both with him!

GREGORY PECK · SUSAN HAYWARD · AVA GARDNER

ERNEST HEMINGWAY'S

THE SNOWS of KILIMANJARO

TECHNICOLOR

20th CENTURY-FOX

with HILDEGARDE NEFF Leo G. Carroll
Torin Thatcher · *Produced by* DARRYL F. ZANUCK · *Directed by* HENRY KING · *Screen Play by* CASEY ROBINSON

THE SNOWS OF KILIMANJARO

Twentieth Century Fox, 1952, colour, release date:
2 February 1953

Producer: Darryl F. Zanuck
Director: Henry King
Screenplay: Casey Robinson
From a short story by Ernest Hemingway
Photography: Leon Shamroy
Music: Bernard Herrman
Running time: 114 minutes

PRINCIPAL CAST

Gregory Peck:	Harry
Susan Hayward:	Helen
Ava Gardner:	Cynthia
Hildegarde Neff:	Liz
Leo G. Carroll:	Uncle Bill

RIDE VAQUERO

MGM, 1953, colour, release date: 7 December 1953

Producer: Stephen Ames
Director: John Farrow
Screenplay: Frank Fenton
Photography: Robert Surtees
Music: Bronislau Kaper
Running time: 91 minutes

PRINCIPAL CAST

Robert Taylor:	Rio
Ava Gardner:	Cordelia Cameron
Howard Keel:	King Cameron
Anthony Quinn:	Jose Esqueda
Kurt Kasznar:	Father Antonio

Mogambo

Mogambo

MOGAMBO

MGM, 1953, colour, release date: 4 January 1953

Producer: Sam Zimbalist
Director: John Ford
Screenplay: John Lee Mahin
Photography: Robert Surtees
Running time: 115 minutes

PRINCIPAL CAST

Clark Gable:	Victor Marswell
Ava Gardner:	Eloise Y. Kelly
Grace Kelly:	Linda Nordley
Donald Sinden:	Donald Nordley

KNIGHTS OF THE ROUND TABLE

MGM, British, 1954, colour and Cinemascope

Producer: Pandro S. Berman
Director: Richard Thorpe
Screenplay: Talbot Jennings, Jan Lustig, Noel Langley
Based on Sir Thomas Malory's *Le Morte d'Arthur*
Photography: F. A. Young, Stephen Dade
Music: Miklos Rozsa
Running time: 115 minutes

PRINCIPAL CAST

Robert Taylor	Lancelot
Ava Gardner:	Guinevere
Mel Ferrer:	King Arthur
Anne Crawford:	Morgan Le Fay
Stanley Baker:	Modred
Felix Aylmer:	Merlin
Maureen Swanson:	Elaine

Knights of the Round Table

Above: Knights of the Round Table
Below: The Barefoot Contessa

"The
World's
Most
Beautiful
Animal!"

HARRY DAWES
Director
" What I tell her to do,
she will do... with her
shoes on that is."

Humphrey
BOGART

Ava
GARDNER

THE
BAREFOOT
CONTESSA

Written and Directed by
JOSEPH L.
MANKIEWICZ
'A Figaro Incorporated Production
UNITED ARTISTS

COLOUR BY **Technicolor** (A)

co-starring EDMOND O'BRIEN · MARIUS GORING
VALENTINA CORTESA · ROSSANO BRAZZI
with WARREN STEVENS · BESSIE LOVE

The Barefoot Contessa

THE BAREFOOT CONTESSA

United Artists, Figaro, 1954, colour, release date:
3 January 1955

Producer: Joseph L. Mankiewicz
Director: Joseph L. Mankiewicz
Screenplay: Joseph L. Mankiewicz
Photography: Jack Cardiff
Music: Mario Nascimbene
Running time: 128 minutes

PRINCIPAL CAST

Humphrey Bogart:	Harry Dawes
Ava Gardner:	Maria Vargas
Edmond O'Brien:	Oscar Muldoon
Marius Goring:	Alberto Bravano
Valentina Cortesa:	Eleanora Torlato-Favrini
Rossano Brazzi:	Vincenzo Torlato-Favrini
Elizabeth Sellars:	Jerry

BHOWANI JUNCTION

MGM, 1956, colour and Cinemascope, release date:
29 October 1956

Producer: Pandro S. Berman
Director: George Cukor
Screenplay: Sonya Levien, Ivan Moffat
From the novel by John Masters
Photography: F. A. Young
Music: Miklos Rozsa
Running time: 110 minutes

PRINCIPAL CAST

Ava Gardner:	Victoria Jones
Stewart Granger:	Colonel Rodney Savage
Bill Travers:	Patrick Taylor

Bhowani Junction

Bhowani Junction

Above: Bhowani Junction
Below: The Little Hut

THE LITTLE HUT

MGM, 1957, colour, release date: 18 November 1957

Producer: F. Hugh Herbert, Mark Robson
Director: Mark Robson
Screenplay: F. Hugh Herbert
From the play by André Roussin
Photography: F. A. Young
Music: Robert Farnon
Running time: 90 minutes

PRINCIPAL CAST

Ava Gardner: Lady Susan Ashlow
Stewart Granger: Sir Philip Ashlow
David Niven: Henry Brittingham-Brett
Walter Chiari: Mario

THE SUN ALSO RISES

Twentieth Century Fox, 1957, colour and Cinemascope,
release date: 30 December 1957

Producer: Darryl F. Zanuck
Director: Henry King
Screenplay: Peter Viertel
From the novel by Ernest Hemingway
Photography: Leo Tover
Music: Hugo Friedhoffer
Running time: 130 minutes

PRINCIPAL CAST

Tyrone Power: Jake Barnes
Ava Gardner: Lady Brett Ashley
Mel Ferrer: Robert Cohn
Errol Flynn   Mike Campbell
Eddie Albert: Bill Gorton

20th Century-Fox presents the love story that was too daring to film until now...

TYRONE POWER · AVA GARDNER
MEL FERRER · ERROL FLYNN
EDDIE ALBERT · JULIETTE GRECO

DARRYL F. ZANUCK'S Production of
ERNEST HEMINGWAY'S

The Sun Also Rises 'A'

EASTMAN COLOUR

1907 1957 HOLLYWOOD GOLDEN JUBILEE

A
CinemaScope
PICTURE
Scope is the registered trade mark of 20th Century-Fox Film Corporation

FEATURING GREGORY RATOFF · MARCEL DALIO · ROBERT EVANS
PRODUCED BY | DIRECTED BY | SCREENPLAY BY
DARRYL F. ZANUCK · HENRY KING · PETER VIERTEL

ARLTON HAYMARKET NOW! | AT YOUR LOCAL CINEMA SOON!

THE NAKED MAJA

*United Artists / Titanus, MGM, 1959, American/Italian,
colour and Technirama, release date: 29 November 1959*

Producer: Goffredo Lombardo
Director: Henry Koster
Screenplay: Giorgio Prosperi, Norman Corwin, Oscar Saul,
Albert Lewin
From a story by Oscar Saul and Talbot Jennings
Photography: Guiseppe Rotunno
Music: Francesco Lavagnimo
Running time: 112 minutes

PRINCIPAL CAST

Ava Gardner:	Duchess of Alba
Anthony Franciosa:	Francisco Goya
Armedeo Nazzari:	Manuel Goday
Gino Cervi:	King Carlos IV
Lea Padovani:	Queen Maria Luisa
Massimo Serato:	Sanchez

ON THE BEACH

United Artists, 1960, black and white, release date:
14 February 1960

Producer: Stanley Kramer
Director: Stanley Kramer
Screenplay: John Paxton, James Lee Barrett
From the novel by Nevil Shute
Photography: Guiseppe Rotunno
Music: Ernest Gold
Running time: 135 minutes

PRINCIPAL CAST

Gregory Peck:	Dwight Towers
Ava Gardner:	Moira Davidson
Fred Astaire:	Julian Osborne
Anthony Perkins:	Peter Holmes
Donna Anderson:	Mary Holmes

On the Beach

On the Beach

On the Beach

THE ANGEL WORE RED

*MGM, American/Italian, 1960, black and white,
Metroscope*

Producer: Goffredo Lombardo
Director: Nunnally Johnson
Screenplay: Nunnally Johnson
Based on a novel by Bruce Marshall
Photography: Guiseppe Rotunno
Music: Bronislau Kaper
Running time: 99 minutes

PRINCIPAL CAST

Ava Gardner:	Soledad
Dirk Bogarde:	Arturo Carrera
Joseph Cotten:	Hawthorne
Vittorio De Sica:	General Clave

55 DAYS AT PEKING

Rank Film Distributors, 1963, colour, 70mm Super Technirama

Producer: Samuel Bronston
Director: Nicholas Ray
Screenplay: Philip Yordon, Bernard Gordon
Photography: Jack Hildyard
Music: Dimitri Tiomkin
Running time: 154 minutes

PRINCIPAL CAST

Charlton Heston:	Major Matt Lewis
Ava Gardner:	Baroness Natalie Ivanoff
David Niven:	Sir Arthur Robertson
Flora Robson:	Dowager Empress Tzu Hsi
Elizabeth Sellars:	Lady Sarah Robertson
John Ireland:	Sergeant Harry
Harry Andrews:	Father de Bearn
Leo Genn:	General Jung-Lu
Robert Helpmann:	Prince Tuan
Kurt Kasznar:	Baron Sergei Ivanoff
Paul Lukas:	Dr Steinfeld
Alfred Lynch:	Gerald

SEVEN DAYS IN MAY

Paramount, Seven Arts Production, 1964, black and white

Producer: Edward Lewis
Director: John Frankenheimer
Screenplay: Rod Serling
Based on the novel by Fletcher Knebel, Charles Bailey II
Photography: Ellsworth Fredricks
Music: Jerry Goldsmith
Running time: 120 minutes

PRINCIPAL CAST

Burt Lancaster:	General James M. Scott
Kirk Douglas:	Colonel Martin 'Jiggs' Casey
Fredric March:	President Jordan Lyman
Ava Gardner:	Eleanor Holbrook
Edmond O'Brien:	Senator Raymond Clark
Martin Balsam:	Paul Girard

THE NIGHT OF THE IGUANA

MGM, 1964, black and white, release date: 5 October 1964

Producer: Ray Stark
Director: John Huston
Screenplay: Anthony Veiller, John Huston
From the play by Tennessee Williams
Photography: Gabriel Figueroa
Music: Benjamin Frankel
Running time: 125 minutes

PRINCIPAL CAST

Richard Burton:	Rev. T. Lawrence Shannon
Ava Gardner:	Maxine Faulk
Deborah Kerr:	Hannah Jelkes
Sue Lyon:	Charlotte Goodall
Grayson Hall:	Judith Fellows
Cyril Delevanti:	Nonno
James 'Skip' Ward:	Hank

THE BIBLE

Twentieth Century Fox, Italian, 1966, colour and 70mm Panavision

Producer: Dino De Laurentiis
Director: John Huston
Screenplay: Christopher Fry
Photography: Guiseppe Rotunno
Music: Toshero Mayuzumi
Running time: 174 minutes

PRINCIPAL CAST

Michael Parks:	Adam
Ulla Bergryd:	Eve
Richard Harris:	Cain
John Huston:	Noah/Narrator
Stephen Boyd:	Nimrod
George C. Scott:	Abraham
Ava Gardner:	Sarah
Peter O'Toole:	The Three Angels

Mayerling

MAYERLING

Associated British/Warner-Pathé, colour and Panavision, release date: 5 October 1970

Producer: Robert Dorfman
Director: Terence Young
Screenplay: Terence Young
From the novel by Claude Anet
Photography: Henri Alekan
Music: Francis Lai
Running time: 140 minutes

PRINCIPAL CAST

Omar Sharif:	Crown Prince Rudolph
Catherine Deneuve:	Maria Vetsera
James Mason:	Emperor Franz Joseph
Ava Gardner:	Empress Elizabeth
James Robertson Justice:	Edward Prince of Wales
Genevieve Page:	Countess Larisch

TAMILIN (The Devil's Widow)

American International, 1972 colour and Panavision

Producer: Alan Ladd Jr, Stanley Mann
Director: Roddy McDowall
Screenplay: William Spier
Photography: Billy Williams
Music: Stanley Myers
Running time: 107 minutes

PRINCIPAL CAST

Ava Gardner:	Michaela
Ian McShane:	Tom
Stephanie Beacham:	Janet
Cyril Cusack:	Vicar
Richard Wattis:	Elroy

THE LIFE AND TIMES OF JUDGE ROY BEAN

National General, 1973, colour

Producer: John Foreman
Director: John Huston
Screenplay: John Milius
Photography: Richard Moore
Music: Maurice Jarre
Running time: 120 minutes

PRINCIPAL CAST

Paul Newman:	Judge Roy Bean
Jacqueline Bisset:	Rose Bean
Ava Gardner:	Lily Langtry
Tab Hunter:	Sam Dodd
John Huston:	Grizzly Adams
Stacy Keach:	Bad Bob
Roddy McDowall:	Frank Gass
Anthony Perkins:	Rev LaSalle
Victoria Principal:	Marie Elena

Earthquake

Earthquake

EARTHQUAKE
Universal, 1974, colour and Panavision

Producer: Mark Robson
Director : Mark Robson
Executive Producer: Jennings Lang
Screenplay: George Fox
Photography: Philip Lathrop
Music: John Williams
Running time: 129 minutes

PRINCIPAL CAST

Charlton Heston:	Stuart Graff
Ava Gardner:	Remy Graff
George Kennedy:	Lew Slade
Lorne Green:	Sam Royce
Genevieve Bujold:	Denise Marshall
Richard Roundtree:	Miles Quade
Marjoe Gortner:	Jody
Barry Sullivan:	Stockle
Lloyd Nolan:	Dr Vance
Victoria Principal:	Rosa

PERMISSION TO KILL
Columbia/Warner, 1976, colour and Panavision

Producer: Paul Mills
Director: Cyril Frankel
Screenplay: Robin Estridge
From his own novel
Photography: Freddie Young
Running time: 96 minutes

PRINCIPAL CAST

Dirk Bogarde:	Alan Curtis
Ava Gardner:	Katina Peterson
Bekim Fehmiu:	Alexander Diakim
Timothy Dalton:	Charles Lord

Permission to Kill

Permission to Kill

THE BLUEBIRD

Edward Lewis Productions, USA, Len Films, USSR, 1976, distributed by Twentieth Century Fox, colour

Executive Producer: Edward Lewis
Producer: Paul Maslansky, Alexander Archansky
Co-producers: Lee Savin, Paul Radin
Director: George Cukor
Screenplay: . Hugh Whitmore, Alfred Hayes, Alexel Kapler
Based on the story by Maurice Maeterlinck
Photography: Freddie Young, Jonas Gritzus
Music: Irwin Kostal, Lionel Newman, Andrei Petrov
Running time: 100 minutes

PRINCIPAL CAST

Elizabeth Taylor:	Mother/Maternal Love/Witch/Light
Jane Fonda:	Night
Ava Gardner:	Luxury
Cicely Tyson:	Cat
Robert Morley:	Father Time
Harry Andrews:	Oak
Mona Washbourne:	Grandmother
Will Geer:	Grandfather
George Cole:	Dog
Nadejda Pavlova:	The Bluebird
Patsy Kensit:	Mytyl
Todd Lookinland:	Tyltyl

THE CASSANDRA CROSSING

Avco Embassy, Anglo/Italian, 1977, colour and Panavision

Producers: Sir Lew Grade, Carlo Ponti
Executive Producer: Giancarlo Pettini
Director: George Pan Cosmatos

Screenplay: Tom Mankiewicz, Katy Cosmatos
From a story by Robert Katz
Photography: Ennio Guarnieri
Music: Jerry Goldsmith
Running time: 126 minutes

PRINCIPAL CAST

Sophia Loren: Jennifer
Richard Harris: Chamberlain
Ava Gardner: Nicole
Burt Lancaster: Mackenzie
Martin Sheen: Navarro
Ingrid Thulin: Elana

The Cassandra Crossing

THE SENTINEL

Universal, 1977, colour, distributed by CIC

Producer: Michael Winner, Jeffery Konvitz
Director: Michael Winner
Screenplay: Michael Winner, Jeffery Konvitz
From a story by Jeffery Konvitz
Photography: Dick Kratina
Music: Gil Melle
Running time: 92 minutes

PRINCIPAL CAST

Cristina Raines: Alison Parker
Chris Saranden: Michael Lerman
Martin Balsam: Professor
John Carradine: Father Halliran
Ava Gardner: Miss Logan
Arthur Kennedy: Franchino
Jose Ferrer: Robed Figure
Burgess Meredith: Charles Chazen
Eli Wallach: Detective Inspector Gatz

**ALL HELL WILL BREAK LOOSE
WHEN THE SENTINEL ARRIVES**

'ROSEMARY'S BABY and THE EXORCIST have prepared the
way for THE SENTINEL, a notably nasty essay into
possession by evil forces, the power of Satan, the legion of
the damned . . . Mr Konvitz writes with efficient and
practised ease.'
Observer

A MICHAEL WINNER FILM

THE
SENTINEL

CHRIS SARANDON CRISTINA RAINES

MARTIN BALSAM   JOHN CARRADINE   JOSE FERRER
AVA GARDNER   ARTHUR KENNEDY   BURGESS MEREDITH
SYLVIA MILES   DEBORAH RAFFIN   ELI WALLACH
Screenplay by MICHAEL WINNER & JEFFREY KONVITZ
Based on the novel by JEFFREY KONVITZ
Music by GIL MELLE
Directed by MICHAEL WINNER
Produced by MICHAEL WINNER & JEFFREY KONVITZ
A UNIVERSAL PICTURE
TECHNICOLOR
Distributed by Cinema International Corporation

Star

The ultimate
intrusion
of evil

Star

THE SENTINEL   Jeffrey Konvitz

THE
SENTINEL

JEFFREY KONVITZ

CITY ON FIRE

Sandy Howard-Astral Bellevue Pathé, 1980, colour

Executive Producer: Sandy Howard, Harold Greenberg
Producer: Claude Heroux
Director: Alvin Rakoff
Screenplay: Jack Hill
Photography: Rene Verzier
Music: William McCauley
Running time: 101 minutes

PRINCIPAL CAST

Henry Fonda:	Fire Chief
Susan Clark:	Diana
Ava Gardner:	Maggie
Barry Newman:	Frank Whitman
Shelley Winters:	Nurse
Leslie Nielson:	Mayor
Richard Donat:	Captain
James Franciscus:	Jimbo

THE KIDNAPPING OF THE PRESIDENT

Sefel Pictures. A Joseph Sefel Production, Bordeaux International, 1981, colour and Panavision

Producer: George Mendeluk, John Ryan
Executive Producer: Joseph Sefel
Director: George Mendeluk
Screenplay: Richard Murphy
Based on the book by Charles Templeton
Photography: Michael Malloy, BSc
Music: Paul Zaza
Running time: 113 minutes

PRINCIPAL CAST

William Shatner:	Jerry O'Connor
Hal Holbrook:	President of the USA
Ava Gardner:	Beth Richards
Van Johnson:	Ethan Richards
Miguel Fernandes:	Roberto Assanti
Elizabeth Shepherd:	The First Lady

PRIEST OF LOVE

*Filmways Pictures Inc.–Enterprise Pictures Ltd,
1982, colour*

Producer: Miles and Andrew Donally
Director: Christopher Miles
Screenplay: Alan Plater
Based on the book *The Priest of Love* by Harry T. Moore,
and Lawrence's own writings and letters
Photography: Ted Moore
Running time: 125 minutes

PRINCIPAL CAST

Ian McKellan:	D. H. Lawrence
Janet Suzman:	Frieda Lawrence
Ava Gardner:	Mabel Dodge Luhan
Penelope Keith:	The Hon. Dorothy Brett

ACKNOWLEDGEMENTS

The author and publishers would like to thank the following film companies for the photographs which appear in this book: Metro-Goldwyn-Mayer, Twentieth Century Fox, United Artists, Universal, Warner Brothers and the National Film Archives Stills Library.

BIBLIOGRAPHY

Ava – Portrait of a Star by David Hanna
(Anthony Gibbs and Phillips, London, 1960)

Ava by Charles Higham
(W. H. Allen, London, 1974)

INDEX

215

216

217

218

219

220